THE EDGE

Nachman Seltzer

TARGUM/FELDHEIM

First published 2004

ISBN 1-56871-301-1

Published by:
TARGUM PRESS, INC.
22700 W. Eleven Mile Rd.
Southfield, MI 48034
E-mail: targum@netvision.net.il
Fax: 888-298-9992
www.targum.com

Distributed by:
FELDHEIM PUBLISHERS
202 Airport Executive Park
Nanuet, NY 10954

Printed in Israel

To Aliza

אשת נעורי

ACKNOWLEDGMENTS

My thanks to...

Hashem for the *siyata diShmaya* that helped me through every step of the way.

Mommy and Tatty for all your help in this and every other facet of our lives.

Grandma Feigy — without you there wouldn't have been a book.

Mommy and Daddy — for all the moral support.

Yael and Adina — for being such yummy little things.

Rav Berkovits, whose clarity in the *inyan* that this book dealt with is as clear as it is in every other one.

The *kollel* — for the unabated interest, although it could get tiresome at times, and the brilliant ideas which added much spice to our daily conversations, such as "Make sure to get the book put in *cherem*." To all the boys, thanks.

Box — for always believing. Just remember Darje's time will yet come.

The staff of Targum Press and especially Miriam Zakon — for all the work you put in to make this book what it is.

My wife Aliza — if I begin to thank you here, it will fill another whole book, so I'll settle for dedicating this book to you.

Prologue

Teveriah, Israel

The funeral was heavily attended, the old and dusty room full of people from many different segments of society. On the right side of the room stood the deceased's four sons: the two older ones in their Chassidic garb, surrounded by sons whose long curly earlocks complemented their rosy cheeks; the third son, Nafti, who was completely bareheaded; and the youngest, Yaakov, with his knitted *kippah* and his boys in shorts. On the left side of the room stood the women of the family: the grieving widow, her older daughters-in-law in modest head scarves and their daughters with braided hair, her daughters in pants and sleeveless blouses, brazenly flaunting the modest dress code of those around them.

The daughters' husbands, nice irreligious chaps from kibbutzim who'd had nothing to do with the patriarch of the family, stood uneasily near their brothers-in-law. Like Nafti, they were bareheaded.

Nafti was short for Naftali — the third son of the family, the one for whom all the cheder rebbeim had predicted a brilliant future in the tents of Torah. He had progressed steadily, immersing himself in his learning, and many times it had been said that this boy would become a *gadol hador*.

On the morning of his eighteenth birthday Naftali packed his bags, threw away his long coat and tzitzis, and cut off his earlocks. He left home and made his way to the closest army base to his house. His tefillin were left at home.

The winds of destruction were blowing across Eretz Yisrael. The *yishuv* in Teveriah lost many of its best children to the kibbutzim.

Within a year Nafti's younger sister Goldie followed his example, changing her name to Zehava and enlisting in the army. This created a stronger and more lasting rift in the family.

Yaakov didn't completely turn his back on the Torah, but he did attend the army and later university, exchanging the traditional Chassidic dress for the more casual Mizrachi look.

Little children look up to and try to emulate their older siblings, so it wasn't a big surprise when Shoshi HaKetanah, or "small Shoshi," as she was known, followed her brother and sister's footsteps and enlisted in the army as soon as she was old enough.

Their mother watched all this happen to her beloved family and tore *keriah* not once but three times. Unfortunately, her illustrious husband wasn't there by her side to comfort her and wipe her tears.

No, he hadn't been there for her in his lifetime, and now once again she was standing alone with a ripped garment and overflowing eyes.

The Heavenly Court

The case of the heavenly hosts versus Reb Yehuda Frankel took place the morning after his *levayah* in the main courtroom of the Beis Din Shel Maalah. Reb Yehuda was escorted down the corridors of Heaven, his dread growing stronger every second.

Every bad deed he'd ever done was coming back to haunt him at this crucial moment. He entered the judgment hall, whose awesomeness bespoke the solemnness of the moment.

Reb Yehuda looked around at the audience sitting and waiting for the trial to commence. He recognized all of them. There was his father, now gone for over twenty years, his face glowing with an otherworldly light. His grandfathers — in fact, all his ancestors — were in attendance, judging him along with the judges.

The angel in white got up to speak. He gave a detailed list of all the good deeds that Reb Yehuda had done, the countless hours of learning accumulated. He eloquently described his devotion to all the mitzvos and his kindness to his fellowman. He waxed poetic as he related to the spectators how beloved Reb Yehuda had been in the community. A tzaddik, a righteous man. A jewel in *klal Yisrael*'s crown.

The faces of his ancestors shone with pride, and Reb Yehuda felt some hope.

Oh, no! What was this?! A fearful looking angel dressed in black was taking the witness stand. He was holding something in his hand. What was it? A soldier's cap? Why was the angel holding a soldier's cap?

The knot in Reb Yehuda's stomach was threatening to engulf him. The angel lifted the offending article in his right hand, and in a ringing voice he began to speak.

True, he conceded, there were many beautiful character traits to be found in the defendant. However, there was one aspect of his life which would not stand up under close inspection. Here he paused for effect and then continued, "The way he treated his family was inexcusable."

He was so busy with all of Teveriah's many widows and orphans, he ran to do *chesed*, to build the sick man's sukkah, and to clothe the poor. How was it possible that he had no time for his own children? Why was such a gifted student like his son Naftali able to roam forbidden roads and to graze in strange pastures?

Why was he not there to comfort his wife, to lend a hand, and to ease the burden of her sorrow? How had he been able to learn in his study in peace and tranquility, while those around him were suffering? Why did he not change his ways after one child had strayed, in order to save the others from hurling themselves off the cliff in pursuit?

He had been derelict in his responsibilities, and look at the results! The angel held up the cap. "Reb Yehuda," he thundered, "how did you not stand up and take notice when your Naftali left the holy walls of the yeshivah to embrace the secular world?

"How did you ignore all this, leaving your *rebbetzin* alone in her misery? There is a judge and there is justice, and I demand a punishment for the accused before he be allowed to enter Gan Eden."

The judges deliberated for a long while. Reb Yehuda sat in silence, expecting the worst. Finally the verdict was announced. The Av Beis Din spoke: "Since you were found lacking in the area of family, Reb Yehuda ben Shamai, you will return to earth to fix these shortcomings.

"The challenges presented to you this time around will be in the area of family; in the area of marriage and children.

"We of the Heavenly Court wish you great success in rectifying your past errors and hope you will return to us clean, pure, and ready for the spot in Gan Eden which awaits you. *Hatzlachah rabbah.*"

Chapter One

Illinois, Great Lakes Region

My sailboat, known affectionately as Kelly, swiftly made its way down the lake. It was Friday night, and I was going to a party at Estelle's house. The shadows were deepening across the lake as the sun sank lower in the sky. The wind blew my hair back and drops of water sprayed my face. I felt really good.

I've been in love with boats and the water for as long as I can remember. I like playing the piano, and I enjoy a good game of ice hockey, but there's nothing that thrills me as much as boating.

My name is Keith Caseman. I live off the lake in a big old house that my parents bought years ago. My dad, who is really good with his hands, renovated the whole house from top to bottom. He painted, sanded, built additional rooms, and ended up with a colossal, rambling home with a deck that ends right by the lake. When I was younger, the fresh air coming in off the lake would wake me up early. I'd throw on some clothes and run down to the dock, jump into my little rowboat, and row for an hour before breakfast.

I graduated to sailboats at around fifteen, and soon I almost lived in my boat. If my mother needed me, the first place she'd look was the lake. Chances were I was there, either with a friend or by myself, fishing or just sailing out to the empty spaces.

Tonight I was in a rush, because when one of your best friends makes a party you want to be on time, especially if she's a Maxwell and her family is one of the classiest ones in town. Estelle was a nice girl, not too stuck up, which in her social circle was a rarity. She liked me, in part because I was a cool guy, but more so because I was so proficient with a boat, which in our town was impressive.

As I neared the Maxwells' property I could hear music playing, and the pinpoints of lights gradually developed into proper beachfront lights, some pink, some white. This was a special party that Estelle was throwing for our class, and everyone was sure to come, even Jim Murray and Steven Gilders who lived out and away. We were nearing the end of our senior year, the summer was approaching, and the realization that we wouldn't be together too much longer was hitting us hard. We came from sheltered, comfortable homes, and inside we were little kids who weren't really ready to face the big, scary world. So we celebrated, pushing the fears down to a place where they wouldn't be seen.

The gazebo on the lawn was bathed in bright lights, each a different color, reflected in the eyes of the kids dancing on the beautiful lawn. A long circular bar ran alongside the garden, with two bartenders serving drinks and a table of hot and cold dishes. As usual, the Maxwells had done a perfect job.

My class was predominately white and Christian, with a couple of blacks and a few Jewish kids like me thrown in. We never discussed religion, though, so what did I care?

My boat moved gracefully up to the dock, where the boy who was hired for the evening took over from me. I stepped out of the boat and ran my hand through my windblown blond hair. I knew I looked good in my white polo shirt, khaki shorts, and sandals.

An excited and sparkling-eyed Estelle came running down to the dock, squealing with delight. "Hi, Keith," she shrieked, handing me a drink. Together, we made our way up the stairs she had just run down. We really were happy that night. If I had known then how much pain I'd have in the future, I don't think I would have had the courage to go on. But I guess that's what good about life — you never know what's going to happen.

More and more kids arrived. Everyone was having a good time, some dancing, some milling around the bar, and some trying their hand at the mike, singing. After a while, we drifted over to the tables, which were covered with big umbrellas. The white wicker chairs sparkled in the bright lights. Joke followed joke, and laughter spilled out over the water.

The band started playing a slow song, one of my favorites, and before I knew it I was being propelled up to the makeshift stage, the lights illuminating my face. I was one of the best singers of the class. I let my voice melt into the mike, alternately sweetly crooning and letting my voice ring out into the depths of the lake. The song gradually reached its climax, and before the band could move into another one, Estelle took another microphone and asked for silence.

The laughter died down and everyone turned to Estelle. She waited for total silence, looked around, met each pair of eyes, and then started speaking. "Thank you for coming tonight. As you know, I don't usually make parties...."

Everyone had a good laugh at that, since Estelle made a party around once a year.

Estelle waited until it was quiet again. "I made this party tonight for two reasons. Well, actually three reasons. Number one, I love parties. Number two, I think we as a group and as individuals are missing out on something very important these last few months of our senior year. This is a time for us to come together as a class and to enjoy our last couple of months together. Let's stop pretending it's not happening. Let's get together more; let's discuss it and not ignore it."

Estelle's big blue eyes were opened wide, and she was gesturing with her hands. The class watched her, most of the girls and even some of the boys nodding in agreement. I had known she felt strongly this, but I was totally unprepared for what she said next.

"Lastly," said Estelle, suddenly turning to look at me, "I wanted to publicly wish my friend Keith much luck in his upcoming sailing competition, which will begin next month. Keith was one of the best junior finalists in the Great Lakes area and was chosen to compete in the contest." There was a buzz from the class. They hadn't even known that I had applied, much less that I was chosen to compete in this high-level contest, which was sponsored by leading manufacturers.

Estelle turned around and walked to the back of the stage to pick up a gaily wrapped package that had been sitting on a little table. She walked back to me and handed me the package with a flourish.

I took it and asked, "You want me to open it now?"

"Please," she said.

I unwrapped the package and opened the fancy leather watch case inside. A gleaming watch sat nestled in satin.

"It's waterproof," said Estelle, "perfect for sailboat racing. It will be your good luck charm. When you wear it, you'll know we're thinking of you and hoping you win every one of those races."

The band started a song and the class burst into applause. I was overcome by happiness that I had such good friends, yet at the same time I felt sad that our school years were almost over. Some other feelings floated around inside me, but I couldn't name them. I realized vaguely that things would soon be totally different, and I should hold onto my familiar life as long as I could.

Chapter Two

The day I was due to leave my parents took me out for breakfast, so that, as my mother put it, she could feast her eyes on her beautiful boy for a little bit longer. I didn't mind, since I'm game for a solid meal, whenever, wherever, and however. We drove out of our property, turning right when we got to the crossroad, and followed Route 33 for about fifteen minutes before hitting the main street. The tall oaks, which had lived in the neighborhood for over a hundred years, stood as strong and as proud as an army, their leaves waving cheerfully at us as my father drove our Jeep Cherokee down the country roads. My mother kept flipping through the channels looking for some good music. We finally settled on one of her favorite songs, "The Ballad of Billy the Kid."

My father, Gene Caseman, hadn't always worked down here. At one point he had been a very high-powered accountant working in an influential Boston firm where he was junior partner. He had been living a very stressful existence and developed a few ulcers. By the time he was thirty, he looked forty-five and was a shell of what he'd once been. There he was, washed up, old before his time, irritable, and not interested in anything

but making money, when my mother just walked, literally, into his life.

He had been on his way out of the office to an important meeting and bent down to tie his shoe by the door. When he stood up she walked right into him. She hadn't noticed him bending down because she'd been looking for the correct office. My father growled, more from sympathy than anger, "Lady, why don't you watch where you're going?"

My mother, Joannie, who doesn't really have the calmest temper in the world, for some reason looked up at him and saw that he could become a whole man again. She picked herself up and asked, "Are you okay?"

My father, so taken aback that she wasn't angry at him, said, "I'm so sorry I knocked you down. Please let me take you out to lunch to make up for being so rude." My mother accepted and they spent a memorable four-hour lunch together, easily my father's longest meal ever.

My father had been recommended to my mother as an accountant and she had been on her way to him when they bumped into each other. My father, after telling the story, always leaned back in his chair with a satisfied smile and said, "I may have missed my meeting that Monday, but I gained a new life."

The truth is, not all of their life together was so easy, since my mother's first husband Kenny would come around a lot in the beginning trying to get my mother to come back to him. Eventually he stopped coming, but it took a lot out of all concerned.

My mother worked as a fashion consultant. She often worked on movie sets, and when I was young I would accompany her sometimes. We used to have really nice times together at home, too, and sometimes she would come out with me in my boat. Now, as we parked right by our favorite place for breakfast, she wasn't smiling, and I knew she was missing me already. She was a little worried about me, too, even though she wouldn't admit it.

We went in, sat down, and chatted to each other about my trip. I would be traveling to England, Sweden, and Israel for the three stages of the contest.

My mother unfolded her napkin and looked at me, her eyes troubled. "Where in Israel will the race take place, Keith?"

"On the Mediterranean," I said, "near Rosh HaNikrah."

"Interesting," mused my mother. "Is that near any religious communities?"

"I really wouldn't know, Mom," I said. "You know I'm not the least bit religious."

"I know," she said, "but those rabbis have a way of getting to a person who's not at all inclined to religion, and before he knows it, suddenly he's brainwashed and walking around with long fringes on his shirt and a huge skullcap on his head!" Her voice started to rise and the people at the next table looked up at us.

I was very surprised, to put it mildly. My mother rarely let things that had nothing to do with her get to her. "I don't think I will have contact with any religious Jews while I'm there, Mom," I said, trying to calm her down.

"Promise me!" she ordered.

This was so bizarre that I couldn't even begin to relate to it. I was going to a sailing contest and my normally calm and accepting mother was making me promise not to have anything to do with religious Jews in Israel, as if they were the devil. Even as I promised her, I hoped I'd run into one or two of them just to make sure they were human.

The waiter's arrival helped to dispel the tension. He unloaded bagels, eggs, and waffles onto the table. Then he brought over a tall cup of decaf for Dad, an orange juice for Mom, and an ice coffee for me. We ate, laughed, took some pictures, and checked out my new waterproof watch. All in all, it was a really enjoyable meal.

In the afternoon I packed my clothes and sailing gear. Obviously, I wouldn't be sailing my boat, but I had a lot of experience with sailing and that didn't faze me. Since my flight was at eight o'clock that evening, I had some time to meet Estelle and say good-bye.

I drove down to her place to pick her up, and we spent a pleasant hour just driving around aimlessly. She got pretty emotional, of course, and said I just better make sure to come back here in one piece and not get into any accident over there.

"Over where?" I asked.

"In Israel," she replied.

"Why is everyone so afraid of Israel?" I wanted to know. "Boating accidents happen everywhere!"

"It's not boating I'm worried about, Keith," she said seriously. "It's those crazy Arabs."

I reassured her that I'd stay far away from Arabs, but inside I was starting to get nervous. Why was everyone so uptight about my going? It was almost as if they had a premonition that something bad was going to happen to me. *Don't get carried away*, I told myself and assured Estelle that all would be fine. Then I pulled a little box from my pocket and gave it to her. She opened it to find a beautiful ring in the shape of a dolphin, an animal she's crazy about.

"Wow, Keith, thank you so much." A tear was forming in the corner of her eye, and I, not being such an emotional sort, figured it was the ideal time to head home.

At six o'clock Mom and Dad drove me to the airport with my luggage. I was excited to be going and planned to have a great time. As for religious Jews, I wouldn't have minded bumping into one or two of them.

Chapter Three

The seven-hour flight to England was uneventful. I am not a great flyer, but our pilot was so good that I almost didn't feel the landing in Heathrow. When I walked out of customs, I saw a distinguished-looking gentleman in a white shirt and bow tie holding a sign that said "Keith Caseman."

I walked over and introduced myself. The man was a driver who would take me and the other kids who had just flown in to the hotel where we'd be staying. A group of kids had already assembled. We waited for another one and then left the building together. Our hotel was a luxurious, old-style building with wrought-iron railings, plush couches, uniformed elevator boys, and a gleaming bar complete with a moose head with antlers.

I was shown to a room which I would share with two other boys, Bart King and Larry MacElwood. We became buddies immediately and decided to tour around together the next day, the day before the race. We ate dinner that night at an excellent restaurant, and I felt very grown up to be in London by myself, having a beer and enjoying the London night life.

Bright and early the next morning we got on the underground. Since none of us had ever been to London before, we got lost a number of times before we finally made it to Madame Toussad's, the famous wax museum. We took pictures with our favorite models and then made it to the palace just in time for the changing of the guards, after which we saw the Tower of London, Big Ben, and the Parliament building. At this point we had enough and took a cab back to our hotel, exhausted from our long day. We got a good night's sleep in preparation for the next day.

The morning of the race dawned gray and cloudy. The hotel staff kept saying, "What a nice day!" and we regarded them with sympathy. We boarded a bus that would take us to the lake where we would race, which was around thirty miles out of London.

The lake was big, stretching for miles. Finally we arrived at the starting point. People were milling around, and there was a festive mood in the sullen air. The lake was surrounded by tall trees whose branches seemed to shoo us away, as if they were saying, "Today of all days you want to race?" There were streamers strung from tree to tree, but I hardly noticed them. My eyes were focused on the main attraction — Lazer 420 sailboats, the sailboats most suited for this kind of racing.

Sparkling clean, each a different color, they were lined up in rows. Each boat had a number. Their sails were unfurled, and they looked ready to go on a voyage to a foreign land. The one thing I wasn't very thrilled about was the fact that the waters were very choppy. The waves kept hitting the shore with tremendous force, and every wave seemed to say, "Come and get me, see if you can!" I will, just wait, I thought.

We each received a life jacket with a number on it. I was number twelve. We stepped into our boats, each of us getting a feel for our particular craft's movement. We jockeyed into position, each boat doing its utmost to outmaneuver the others.

Testing the wind's direction, we surged forward toward the starting line.

A voice from over the loudspeaker filled the air. "Sound of the gun," it said. "On your marks, get ready, get set —" *boom!* We were off!

Immediately boat number three took the lead, not because he was a great sailor but because the water current around the boats pushed him. I didn't try just yet, since I like to wait a little bit to see which way the water is rushing, how the current moves, and other such things, which are often more important than moving as quick as you can. As of now, I was in the middle of the pack.

I grabbed the tiller and let my boat move into the wind, my sail pulled taut. A big wave came just then and I had to jump out of the way to avoid being thrown overboard. The deck was drenched and I thanked Estelle for my waterproof watch. Then suddenly it started to rain — and not just rain. Sheets of water came pouring down and a fog moved in, too. I couldn't see ten feet in front of me. In fact, I could barely see in front of my boat.

My sail was standing straight against the wind, drenched in the rain, and I was standing in a foot of water. There is nothing like standing with your feet underwater, not being able to see three feet ahead of you, with rain pouring down, on a strange lake, in a country you just arrived in! Try it if you don't believe me.

But I had a little trick up my sleeve, literally. My watch had a number of additions I'm sure Estelle hadn't known about when she bought it, one of which was a compass which lit up in the dark. The darker it got, the shinier my watch face became, and with the compass I was able to continue in the right direction. This was a big help, because it was getting much harder to look at my navigation panel. The wind and rain were so strong and steady that I could barely hold on to the tiller.

We wallowed in the water of the lake like drunken sailors.

Up and down we went, lightning cracking through the fog and thunder booming like a giant drum set, played by a heavenly orchestra. You might think I was dying of fear, but strangely it was an exhilarating experience. It was as if I was at the mercy of nature. Whatever would happen, that's what would happen.

Then, just as my boat started heeling over from the tremendous amount of water inside it, the fog lifted, and I could see that I was miraculously still on course. Not only that, I was only about a hundred yards from the finish. But I wasn't the only one who was almost at the end.

To my right, plodding determinedly along, was boat number fifteen, the black one, looking like a sea monster or an old pirate ship coming to raid the innocent. Now was the time for action. I moved in his direction, tacking across his course, making him veer out of the way to prevent a collision. I was taking a risk, daring him to continue toward me, neither one of us knowing who would cave in first. I sailed aggressively at him, my prow sending him spinning out of my way and into the shallow area of the lake. He was now totally off course and out of the running.

Ten seconds later I sailed into the finish spot in first place. Flashbulbs popped and journalists yelled questions at me. All I was capable of answering at that time was, "It was all because of this." I held up Estelle's present for all to see and then collapsed on the deck, totally shot.

By this time, other boats were coming in, but the attention was still focused on me. The paramedic who was on hand in case of emergencies pulled me into a warm room nearby. I spent the next couple of hours recovering from my ordeal. When we got back to London that evening, I was more or less back to myself. There was a ceremony in the hotel ballroom to mark the end of the first part of our contest. Journalists from many sports magazines were there, and even *Sports Illustrated* had sent someone to interview me.

His name was Benny, and we had met before. "So," he said to me when we met in the lounge before dinner, "how does it feel to win again?" He'd covered other races that I'd been in.

"Well," I said, "normally it feels great, and I know that if I hadn't handled the boat as well as I did then I wouldn't have won. But today out there on the lake when I almost went overboard and I was hanging onto the tiller with one hand and the ropes with the other, I realized that it had nothing to do with me. I could just as easily have gone right overboard, and in that fog, forget it. No one would have been able to find me! We're like pawns in the hands of a master chess player, and we can't change whatever he wants to happen."

"But Keith," Benny said, crossing one foot over the other and loosening his tie, "wasn't there anything you did that helped you win?"

"Benny," I said, "if not for the present I got from my friend before I left," I gestured to the watch, "I would be a goner. This compass guided me through the fog."

"Well, Keith," said Benny, "I must say you are a refreshing change from the rest of the young sports stars I interview. By them, it's 'Yeah, man, if not for that shot I took from half court or my unbelievable pitching performance,' or 'Did you see when I took him down in the third quarter with that left hook. Yeah, my famous left hook!' " And here Benny started doing imitations of the stuck-up young athletes he often met. I laughed. "You're different," he continued. "You keep on saying that you're not the guy behind your success."

We said good-bye and I went down to dinner in the ballroom.

I sat with Larry and Bart and we discussed the race. They both had gotten off to a bad start, particularly Bart, who told me that when the fog came in he went so off course that he thought he was nearing Scotland! "I probably would have gotten to Scotland, but I hit shore by mistake and decided to say there until the fog lifted. That's why I came in second to last." He rolled his eyes humorously, and we all laughed along with him.

That night I lay in bed thinking over the events of the day, and I remembered how I felt as I was standing in the pouring rain with no control over my destiny and how I knew then that I was just a boat in a pond being controlled by someone above. Until then I had been the type of guy who thought that each person shaped his own life. If you lost, it was only because you weren't trying hard enough. Now I realized it wasn't that. I couldn't put my finger on who was in control, but I was sure I'd figure it out sooner or later.

Two days later *Sports Illustrated* came out with a picture of me on the cover, just out of my boat, standing on the deck soaking wet with hair plastered to my forehead, holding Estelle's watch in my hand. The gold medal was draped across my chest and the caption read, "The all-encompassing fog breaker, Keith Caseman. Read how his watch took him out of the darkness. Story on page seventy-one."

I made sure to send two copies back home, one to my mother and one to Estelle. Meanwhile, we had work to do. We had to practice for our next race in Sweden, which was to take place the following week. For the next couple of days I practiced an hour or two daily.

Finally the big day came. We boarded the British Air flight to Sweden and landed in a very modern airport. Again our driver was waiting for us with a sign, and we were driven to our hotel. A few days were scheduled for touring, which we of course took full advantage of. Then it was time for the race.

This time the water was calm, serene, and nonthreatening. The sky was bright and sunny, with not a cloud in sight, but a brisk wind was blowing. I adjusted my watch on my arm. It felt good there, and I knew it would help me in the race. We got into our boats, and the race began.

I didn't think this race was so important, since I'd won the first one already. If one person won all three races he became the world champion for junior racing, but it was very unlikely that one person would win all the races. If two different people won the first two races, the third race would be the deciding one. Since I was already in a good position, I felt calm and in control. I let my boat go with the flow, my sails getting the full effect of the wind. I used my knowledge of boating to move ahead of some of the guys, but I wasn't in a rush.

The water swirled around the boats, its waves hitting their hulls. Then I realized why they had picked this lake for the race. The water was moving in circles, right? No! The circles were within other circles, surrounded by even more circles. In my mind, that said whirlpool! It wouldn't suck the boats in, but if you didn't know what you were doing it would slow you down considerably.

I saw one boat beginning to turn in a gradual circle and the sailor trying to steer it back on course. But he didn't know that when it comes to whirlpools you can't go against the current. I turned my tiller sharply to the left, away from the ever-widening circles, trying to get my boat to a safe place. I managed to avoid the circles, but the wind was trying its hardest to push me back to them. My sails were putting up a fight. For how long?

Meanwhile, ten boats were going around in circles. Looking at the lake from a helicopter, seeing the boats chasing their tails would have been a funny sight. But we sailors had experienced better humor in our lives. I was stuck between the circles where the other boats were and the wind pushing me back there.

Then I remembered Captain Bob, a grizzled old sailor

whom I had met at Cape Cod one summer. I was sitting on the beach with my parents when he approached. He looked at me from under thickly knitted brows and said, "Boy, the sea is in you. You're at peace with the water, aren't you?"

I said, "Yes."

He said, "Many a night I wished for a young lad such as you to help me around my place."

It was summer, I had plenty of time, and my parents had no objection to my going to help Captain Bob with his boat. He was fiercely independent, but he was also old, so he needed my help. We went boating together for hours at a time, and the knowledge I gained from being around him more than paid me back.

At night he would grill up a trout fresh from the river, and as long as I live I'll never forget the taste of that trout, the smell of fish roasting on the fire, the sight of the cabin shrouded in darkness with the fire throwing shadows on the walls. After we ate we sat around the fire, he smoking a pipe of cherry-flavored tobacco and I chewing a stick of gum, and he would tell stories. Those stories will stay with me for the rest of my life.

The captain knew every corner of the bay. Where the fish grew best, where snapping turtles lived, and where old Eli's sailboat was sunk twelve years before. One afternoon when we were sitting on the lake dozing, the sail blowing in the breeze, the captain yelled, "Keith!"

I awoke with a start. "What, Captain Bob?"

"Come here."

I came. He was standing at the side of the boat and pointing at something. "Do you see that?" he asked me.

"What?"

"That," he replied. "Look, son, look."

It was a giant circle in the water, revolving slowly, and there was another circle within the first one, and another inside that. And they were approaching our boat. He said, "This will be a lesson to you. It may be the most important lesson I've taught you.

"That," he said, his hand still outstretched, "is a whirlpool. Sometimes, like now, they can be big enough to slow you down and move you around with them. Most sailors make mistakes when faced with them. You won't! Watch carefully, Keith. The current will move the boat with the circle if we let it. But we won't. You must use the wind for yourself. Don't let it dominate you. As we go around this time, we will get to the furthest end of the circle with our oars.

"Now the wind is blowing our sails with great force, right, Keith? Right. Good, now leave the sails in their exact position and help me pull the centerboard up into the boat." We hoisted the centerboard up onto the boat's deck. The wind, not having anything to fight against now that the centerboard was pulled up and the boat wasn't offering any resistance, was blowing with great anger. It pushed us so furiously that we were thrown all the way across the circle, straight through all the revolving pools and out the other side.

"There you have it," said Captain Bob that night as we were sitting in his nice, warm cabin, comfortably dry. "That's seamanship at its best."

All this ran through my mind in a split second as I saw the great circle approaching me on this Swedish lake. I was in just the right position, the wind getting wilder and more aggressive every second. Then, right before the circle came up to me, as so many other boats were getting tangled up, I yanked the centerboard up onto my deck and the wind practically threw me across the great expanse of the whirlpool.

I reached the other side, slipping my centerboard down into place, and sailed into a very respectable second place. We all

docked and were helped offshore to a round of applause.

I felt that the races couldn't get more interesting. So far we'd had a storm in the first one and a whirlpool in the second. What else could possibly happen?

Chapter Four

The starkly white plane with the blue star on its tail rose into the heavens, taking us over the clouds to the land of Israel. With a sigh of relief I leaned back in my comfortable first class seat. Most of my group was sleeping off the last few whirlwind days. Some were reading, the overhead lights gleaming in the duskiness of the plane.

A stewardess came around asking if anyone wanted anything to drink. I accepted a little airplane bottle of Jack Daniels and a cup of ice. As I poured the amber-colored liquid over the clear cubes, I replayed my last telephone conversation with Estelle in my mind.

She had loved hearing about how her watch had saved the day back in England, and she was delighted with my rendition of how Captain Bob's advice saved me in Sweden. "So now it's all over and we're on our way to Israel," I concluded.

"Great," she said. "Now I'm going to have to worry about terrorists!"

"If nothing happened to me until now, Estelle, there's a good chance nothing will happen in Israel, no?"

"I don't know, Keith. I have a bad feeling about this trip, as if something's going to happen and you'll never come home, and even if you do come home it'll never be the same again!"

Not owning a crystal ball, there was nothing I could say to that, so I just replied that I wished she would stop being so dramatic and that everything would be just fine!

Now, as I thought things over, though, I was having some doubts. So many things had gone wrong so far. First the unexpected storm, which could have easily washed me overboard, then the whirlpools, which had been positively scary. What would happen now? I wondered.

This was the deciding race, since a different boy had won each of the first two. I wanted very much to win. It would mean money, prestige, and all sorts of nice things. *Anyway*, I said to myself, *thousands of tourists go to Israel each year and there's almost never a problem*.

My thoughts turned to Israel. What kind of a country was it, that it had such a magnetic hold on people all over the world? Although my parents had never been there, my dad always got heated up whenever Israel was discussed on the news. Usually we heard about the savage Israelis who oppressed the poor Palestinians, and Dad would say, "If the Mexicans decided to go to war against America because America took away Texas from them, then America would have every right to defend itself, no? And if they would try to blow up American citizens, America would wipe them out! So why is everyone so obtuse and callow when it comes to this tiny little country about the size of New Jersey?"

The movie screen was on, showing a tourism special about Israel. I put my earphones on and listened as the pictures flashed before me. I was shown modern Tel Aviv and ancient Jaffo side by side, then the Dead Sea where the high-rise hotels stuck out against the background of the rocky beach. There was footage of the gorgeous waters of Eilat with its glass-bottomed boats and dolphin shows. Then came Jerusalem, the capital of Israel and one of its finest cities, with religious spots for everyone.

Somewhere over the ocean I fell asleep to the soun clarinetist I found on one of the music channels as the screen flashed a picture of monks in black cloaks, Arabs with red hats on their heads, and elderly men with long white beards dancing in a circle by a wall covered in leaves vied. The image faded into one of a little boy whose intense coal black eyes peeked out from under his cap and then mixed with the suntanned face of a kibbutz girl picking oranges and the serious form of a young soldier, rifle slung over his shoulder. I dreamt of a land of rivers of milk and honey flowing together through mountain passes where goats frolicked under the shade of verdant palm trees, clusters of dates swaying to and fro in the breeze.

I slept the sleep of the just, waking briefly for a meal and drifting off quickly once again. All at once a language I didn't know was being spoken over the loudspeaker. I woke with a start to hear the captain announcing in Hebrew and then in English that we'd be momentarily landing at Ben Gurion Airport. I rubbed sleep from my eyes, got my stuff together, and prepared for landing.

The first thing I noticed when I got off the plane was the heat. The sun glared brightly off the pavement and off the palm trees standing off to the side. Some of my fellow passengers got down and kissed the ground. I wondered why. A silver-blue bus pulled up to take us to the airport.

We drove up to a building that said "Welcome to Israel" in English, with Hebrew letters opposite. I felt very much at home already. Our base was the Dan Panorama Hotel in Tel Aviv, and we had a week off to tour the country. I knew where I was headed.

As soon as I finished unpacking and had a shower in my room, I packed an overnight bag with a change of clothes, my

Walkman, my tourist guidebook, and some food. Then I was on my way to the Central Bus Station — destination Eilat, home of the bluest water Israel has to offer, or so I'd been told. "The hiking is challenging and there are many water sports available," an Israeli at the airport had told me. It sounded good to me. This time I'd go touring alone. For some reason, I didn't ask any of my new friends to come along.

Directions were easy to get, and I boarded a city bus to the bus station. Since the bus to Eilat was full, I decided to take a bus to Jerusalem and catch a connecting bus to Eilat from there. Once on the bus, I settled down in my seat, my pack under my feet, and pulled out my Walkman. But I didn't feel like listening to music. I felt this need to look out the window and take in my surroundings. We passed through the industrial area of the city, driving beside train tracks and tall high-rise buildings. Then we were on the intercity highway, surrounded first by flat land and then by hills. The land got hillier and rockier as we approached Jerusalem. Within an hour we arrived at the Jerusalem Central Bus Station, where I caught the bus to Eilat as it was pulling out.

I turned to the boy sitting next to me, a soldier who looked only a little older than me. "Excuse me, which areas is this bus going to pass through?"

He replied in very accented English, "The Dead Sea, Ein Bokek, Massada, and then we get to Eilat."

I thanked him and got out my tourist handbook to look up the places.

The Dead Sea sounded like a nice place to visit with its mud treatments and hotels. Ein Bokek didn't seem like anything special. But Massada, that enchanted me. I read the short paragraph of historical background in my guidebook. The mountain had been the Jewish people's headquarters in a rebellion against Rome hundreds of years ago. When the Romans gained upper hand and ascended the mountain, they found all the people dead, having committed suicide to avoid the humiliation of capture. "Today," the paragraph concluded, "Israeli soldiers are taken to Massada, where they are sworn in with the words, 'Massada will never fall again.' "

Wow, I thought to myself, *that's fascinating*. An ancient camp of Jewish people struggling against the most powerful army of its time! And not giving in until the very end! Then and there my next stop became Massada. This was one place I had to see.

Eventually the buildings gave way to fields, flowers smiling up at us as we rode past. The white lines blurred into one, and my eyes closed of their own accord. When I woke up the bus was on a narrow, curving road. On one side was a very solid mountain, and on the other was a small metal gate at the edge of the road, which overlooked a lazy body of water. The water barely moved. I guessed this was the Dead Sea. I imagined having a race in this sea, but because there was no air and no waves I quickly gave up the idea.

We passed hiking trails, beach areas, and then a line of luxury hotels built right off the highway. Drivers coming from the other direction whizzed past us, apparently oblivious to the fact that one false move on this curving road meant hitting a tiny barrier and flying twenty feet down to rocks and water, but it didn't seem to bother anyone. It definitely didn't disturb the Bedouins shepherding their sheep off to the side, their dirty robes threadbare, faces devoid of emotion as they watched the traffic moving past them.

It was the closest mix of two centuries I'd ever seen. Modern society rushed along, chasing that elusive pot of gold, and the old-fashioned folk were content, secure in their way of life, not trying to move anything. "What my father did is what I do," they were saying.

Just then I saw a sign, "Massada — twenty kilometers." Suddenly it hit me — I was traveling to an ancient mountain where warriors had awaited the Romans' arrival. Could this modern bus really take me to that historical site? Didn't the past get pushed away by the present? Not here, it seemed.

My seat mate grinned at me. "Going to Eilat?" he asked.

"Yes," I said, "but not just yet. First I think I'll drop by Massada. What about you? Are you going to Eilat?"

"No, I'm going to my base."

Suddenly, a question occurred to me. "Tell me," I asked, "did you have a ceremony at Massada when you first became a soldier?"

"No," he answered, "they don't do it there anymore. Besides, only the paratroopers used to go and I'm in the air force."

"Wow," I said. "As a kid I dreamed of the air force! What do you do there?"

"I'm a helicopter pilot."

"What's your name?" I asked him.

"Donny," he said. "What's yours?"

"Keith." We shook hands. "It's a pleasure to meet you," I said.

There were still a few minutes left until we got to Massada, so I asked, "Were you ever in danger, Donny?"

"Once," he said, his eyes taking on a far-off look. "A few months ago there were a few big terrorist attacks. The army had to respond forcefully. My unit was put on alert together with the Sayeret Matcal, which is the most elite unit in the army. Like the navy seals in America, maybe.

"First we practiced in a fake Arab village — the Sayeret Matcal went in and we were up in the air for cover. In practice all went well. When we went into Kalkilya things started to go wrong."

"What happened?" I asked.

"Three Apache helicopters went in first to see if anything didn't look the way it should. There was quiet, since a curfew was in force. Everything looked all right and we got the go-ahead for the ground troops. They went in slowly, house to house, making sure to avoid booby traps. We looked out for snipers.

"My best friend, Yaniv..." he paused, then went on, "was lieutenant of the ground troops. He went in first. Suddenly I saw that he was approaching a square-shaped house with a courtyard in the middle of it.

"The courtyard was partly covered, so I couldn't see the entire area, but from the angle I was at, I could see that an ambush was being prepared in that courtyard."

I inhaled slowly at the thought of what Donny must have felt, going through something like this.

"We radioed into control. 'Red alert, ambush! Permission to take them out?' 'Permission denied. Civilians in the vicinity, as well as a school for little children. Do not proceed with your request!' I tried to radio Yaniv of the immediate danger, but there must have been a radio malfunction, since I wasn't able to get through to him. We watched helplessly as the troop walked unknowingly into the arms of snipers, with Yaniv at its head.

"They entered the house and went from room to room, checking for terrorists. I watched as the Arabs in the courtyard set up sandbags with slits for machine guns. Those guns had enough power to cut the platoon to slivers."

I stared at Donny with compassion as he relived the horrible story. "It was only a matter of time," he continued, "until the boys in the house would finish going through it and enter the courtyard. I wasn't about to sit there and watch my best friend get sliced up because some idiot at ground control was making a dumb mistake. I decided to start machine gunning the terrorists. Hopefully Yaniv and the boys would hear a battle going on and stay away from the courtyard.

"I gave the order and we zeroed in on our targets. Just then I saw a sniper on the roof of a building aiming at one of our helicopters. Yaniv started to open the door to the courtyard. There wasn't enough time to start picking off terrorists! I gave an order, and our helicopters went into action. One machine gunned everyone in the open, including the sniper on the roof. The others went up higher and dropped a few knock-out bombs. We took out most of the house.

"Unfortunately, Yaniv didn't emerge unscathed. When they opened the door it triggered an explosion and he suffered multiple wounds, but at least he's still alive. Others weren't as lucky."

My chest felt tight and my eyes started to tear.

"If I would've moved quicker," said Donny, almost to himself, "that sniper wouldn't have gotten anyone. As it was, I heard his bullets whistling around our helicopter. I knew I would be imprisoned for disobeying a direct command, but hey, what kind of guy would I be if I hadn't done anything? This way I can look Yaniv's family in the eye and say I saved his life!"

"How long did you sit for?" I asked Donny.

"Five months. I also went down in rank, but it was worth it. I would do it again in a second if I could. Look out the window up there and to the right, Keith. You see that tremendous mountain? That's Massada. I have a feeling that the soldiers who were fighting back then would've done exactly the same thing!"

I had that feeling, too. As we said good-bye I looked at this guy who had such responsibility on his shoulders in admiration and shook his hand. Then I got off the bus and watched as it rumbled off into the distance.

Looking around, I took in my surroundings. I was standing by a bus stop near the hostel I'd seen in my guidebook, which was nestled at the foot of the mountain. The asphalt looked hot enough to fry an egg on, and the sprinklers in the hostel's gardens were working full force.

A few Japanese tourists were waiting at the bus stop. With much smiling and hand waving, they asked me if I could take a picture of them. I obliged most graciously. Then I decided to check into the hostel before starting up the mountain.

The wooden steps leading up to the office were smooth from the countless pairs of feet which had proceeded me, and I followed the signs to the office. A tall young man who introduced himself as Joel sat behind the desk. He informed me of the checkout times, where the TV and dining room were located, and at what time the bar opened. I paid, took my key, and went to the room.

There were eight beds in the room, four of which were unmade with belongings strewn all over. I picked a bed and sat down with my guidebook. It was already mid-afternoon, and it seemed like a waste of time to go up to the mountain now. I decided to wait until the next morning and go up the snake path before dawn. If I started at four in the morning, the guidebook said, I could hit the top at dawn.

There was a nice atmosphere in the hostel, a feeling of friendliness and of the joy of vacation. It was also much hotter than the cities I had just come from. I took a shower to get rid of my traveling dirt, put on a new T-shirt, and was ready to roam. First I explored the grounds. Then I flipped through the channels of the one and only TV. There was nothing on. I bought a Pepsi from a soda machine and sat down at one of the tables to drink it, hoping something would happen soon.

Before long, a boy walked over to me. He was on the tall side, with blonde hair cut in a crew cut and broad shoulders. "Hello," he said in accented English. "My name is Carl and I am staying here with my parents for the day. We have a car and I was wondering if you'd be interested in checking out the area with us."

I told him I'd be delighted to join them, and he introduced me to his parents, who were older people in their late fifties.

We went down to the parking lot and got into a little rented car. Carl said that he had seen an interesting hike on a map of the area. It was supposedly hard to do but had a great lookout spot, so even if you didn't do the hike it was worth driving there for the view.

"What's the name of the hike?" I asked.

"It's called Darje," he replied.

On the way there we exchanged information with each other. The family's name was Manheim and they were from Germany. The parents had come to visit Carl, who was volunteering at a kibbutz for children with mental disabilities. They were planning on climbing Massada tomorrow also.

Carl took the curves with two fingers resting lightly on the wheel. He looked very comfortable in the driver's seat. His mother didn't seem as comfortable as he was. Every so often she'd look out the window and give a little cry of fear. "Carl, *gei nicht a zei shnel*," she'd exclaim. He just laughed and patted her arm.

About thirty minutes later we saw a sign telling us the next turnoff was ours. The road was steep and rocky, curving and narrow all together. It took all of Carl's driving abilities to keep the car happy. He took the curve slowly, his hand moving from gas to clutch to break. His mother refused to look out the window after she saw the view.

We kept going higher and higher. The cars down below were like little toys. We looked off to the side of the road and saw a panoramic view of the Dead Sea, mountain roads, and kibbutzim. After fifteen minutes of navigating, we reached the summit and got out of the car. I was positive that the drop off this mountain would be fatal.

Carl's parents walked off together and found a seat at one of the lookout areas. Carl and I went for a little stroll to explore the area. There was a caravan up there with a huge antenna, some small houses, and signs indicating the end of the trail that my guidebook called one of the toughest climbs in Israel. What had taken us fifteen to twenty minutes to drive up would have taken an hour and a quarter to walk up. Up here, the roads down below looked like chalk lines on a blacktop, the water to the left of them, the mountains to the right. There was very little vegetation to be found. Only among the houses was there some grass, and once we left that immediate area and walked toward the trails it became rocky and sandy.

Hot air swirled around us as we started descending one of the paths. Carl decided he was uncomfortable and took off his shirt, tying it around his waist. The sunlight shone brightly between the shadows cast by the mountains. The trail started down a mountain ridge which separated the sides of the mountain. On either side of it was a drop of at least fifty feet. I picked my way gingerly, but Carl was a lot more sure-footed.

He held his head high and his back straight, and I could see where the Germans had come up with the concept of the master race. What a physique he had!

A film I had once seen about the Nazis popped into my mind. I remembered scenes from the big Nuremburg rallies, young boys Carl's age clad in black uniforms giving the hated salute. Fifty years before and Carl would've been there, perhaps in the SS, maybe the army.

Suddenly I felt so uncomfortable in this situation that I said, "Carl, let's go back."

He turned to look at me, eyes squinting in the sun's glare, chest hard with muscle, and asked, "You had enough?" I choked out some reply, but all I could see was Carl in a Nazi uniform telling me to go to the left.

The sun was setting slowly as we made our laborious descent down the treacherous road. The sky was purple and red mixed with yellow, and a subdued Carl held the wheel tightly in both hands. His father snored slightly next to me in the back, his head lolling from side to side.

They were such a nice family, and yet I felt claustrophobic in the car with them. I was extremely happy when we were speeding once again down the well-lit Ein Gedi highway. And when the car parked next to the hostel, I thanked Carl with as much sincerity as I could and got out of the car with a sigh of relief.

It was cooler now, and I returned to my room to put on a sweatshirt. Then I went to the dining room for supper. A motley group of people sat around the table. A couple of bus drivers with pot bellies ate heartily next to Scandinavian and German tourists and lots of young Americans like me.

I struck up a conversation with two girls on my left. They were from South Carolina and were in Israel with their pastor, who took a group from his church once a year. They babbled enthusiastically about the great sights they'd seen in Israel so far. Suddenly one turned to the other and said, "Trish, doesn't he look like that sailboat guy from *Sports Illustrated*?"

"Yeah," said the other one, "he does."

"There's a simple reason why I look like him," I said. "I am him."

"Wow, tell us all about that storm!"

I spent a few minutes rehashing my storm. We left the dining room at seven-thirty, and at about eight o'clock the lights by the office went on and a bartender materialized from nowhere. Music starting playing, and I spent an enjoyable few hours singing and relaxing.

My alarm went off at 3:45 the next morning, waking me instantly. I was overcome with excitement, even though I tried telling myself that it was just a mountain and there was no reason for it to affect me so. But then again this wasn't just any mountain. I got dressed quickly, grabbed my backpack, and left the hostel.

The early morning air stung my cheeks and cleared my head of the last vestiges of sleep. I wasn't the only one out so early — a group of guys with backpacks were heading to the foot of the mountain, too. We paid our fees, passed the cable cars, and started up the mountain. The group near me started a song with English words, but I wasn't familiar with all of them. The guys all wore caps, and some had black velvet coverings on their heads.

It was pitch black when we started. Now the sky was slowly getting lighter and the hike was getting a little more strenuous. I was sweating from exertion, but the guys in the group around me were still singing. Some even had guitars strapped to their shoulders. It was hard enough for me to carry a backpack; I couldn't imagine carrying a guitar, too. The higher we got, the lighter the sky became, and soon we could see the view.

As we reached the final stretches of the climb, our breathing became more rapid, and the guys stopped singing. And then as the sun rose over the horizon we could see the cable car station over our heads, and we knew we had reached the summit. *This is it*, I thought, *the battleground of my ancestors*. I was sure everyone would run into the sight.

But wait, what were the boys doing? From their backpacks they were extracting small velvet bags, and from those emerged strange looking objects, black boxes attached to black leather straps, which they proceeded to strap onto their heads and arms. They seemed to be religious objects, but why were they putting them on now? Why didn't they just go onto the mountain?

One boy, noticing my confusion, pulled me to the side and asked, "Excuse me, are you Jewish?"

"Yes," I said, "but I never saw these things before!"

"These are called tefillin and we pray with them."

"Why now?" I asked him.

"It's a great thing to pray when the sun is rising," he said. "I can explain more later."

I sat on the side resting and watched those boys praying on the top of the snake path at the summit of Massada while the sun rose. I could almost hear the voices of Jews of the past echo in the valley in response to their prayers. The boys' sweet voices blended together and touched a chord in my heart that had never been touched before.

After the prayers were over, the guys put the boxes away into their bags, and the boy who had spoken to me before came over again. He introduced himself as Dave and asked me if I wanted to try on the boxes.

I hesitated. "I'll tell you the truth, I never did something like this before."

A few of the other boys were listening. They came over and one said, "Try them on. It'll be good for you. One time won't hurt you!"

My mother's voice came back to me. *Watch out for those rabbis*, it said.

I quieted the voice and let them wind the straps around my arm. Then I repeated a prayer word for word after Dave. For the first time in my life, I felt an incredible feeling of belonging wash over me, the feeling of being part of my people. It was something I had never felt before.

While I was standing there, overcome, the boys had taken some food out of their packs and sat down to eat. Then two of them took out their guitars, and they all sat down in a circle on the floor and started singing. I didn't know any of the songs and

I didn't understand the words, but this music was the sweetest sound I had ever heard!

After spending the morning climbing, singing, and praying for the first time, I was understandably tired and ready for a break. But before I could even think of making my way down the mountain, I had to check out all there was to see.

I looked at all the exhibits and gazed out over the horizon at the desert sand and dry landscape, putting myself into the mind frame of the past. After concentrating for a while I could just about see the men in their colorful robes as they scurried back and forth checking the defenses and getting the hot molten lead ready for pouring down the mountainside.

The women were in makeshift houses stirring pots of food over open fires, holding crying children to their shoulders as they huddled together. The looks on their faces bespoke fear and at the same time pride and defiance. Older children chased each other around the camp laughing as they played some ancient form of tag.

It was evening in my reverie, and down below, very far below, if you looked very carefully and had very good eyesight you could see a column of metal-armored legionnaires moving together up the steep, sloping side of the mountain. An officer on a horse urged them on. He was dressed in metal from head to toe. Even the white horse had some metal covering his back.

It was like watching a movie with no sound. The officer gestured with his hands, his mouth open, but no sound was heard. Up on top of the mountain the children, now subdued, gathered around their mothers, clutching their robes. The men were running from side to side in a frenzy, with buckets of boiling hot lead ready to be poured down the holes in the sides of the walls.

Down below the officer stood up in his stirrups and shook his fists at his men, sending them into battle. The rows of legionnaires stood poised to conquer the stubborn Jews of Judea. Just when they were close enough, a signal was given to the Jews up on top and the lead was poured down the mountainside, where it sizzled on the soldiers' metal helmets and drained off to pool into the cracks of their armor, penetrating their clothing and inflicting pain and agony on the unsuspecting men.

Their mouths opened and silent screams erupted. The men bellowed, seeking comfort from the liquid pain. Some lost control and broke out of the close grouping of soldiers, causing others to lose their balance. As the more agile soldiers jumped out of the way, the less coordinated found themselves being pushed over the side.

Since no amount of yelling from the officer on his horse changed the situation, he turned his horse around to retreat. Then a helmet hit him. Taken by surprise, he lost control, tumbled off his horse, and rolled down into the gaping abyss hundreds of feet below.

The soldiers, seeing the officer fall, turned tail and ran down the mountainside in disarray. Up above on the summit of Massada I imagined the now happy families sitting together, having averted disaster once again. But for how long, that was the question.

Suddenly my thoughts were interrupted by a tap on my shoulder. It was Dave. "We're leaving now. Do you want to come down in the cable car with us?" he asked.

Accepting the invitation, I said a quiet farewell to the ghosts of Massada and joined his group.

Chapter Five

My trip to Eilat was the antithesis of my Massada adventure. The bus pulled into Eilat's Central Bus Station as evening fell and neon lights were turning on all around us. Bars beckoned invitingly, brightly lit hotels with names like David, Solomon, and Herod lined the streets, tourists came and went at all hours. The night life was great, but an integral component was missing from its heart.

The waterfront looked very inviting, yachts slowly floating away from the dock. The casino boat was full of people trying to make their fortune. I took all the frenzy in and concluded that I missed the quiet realness, the solidness of the mountain I'd just come from.

I won't tell you I didn't enjoy the next few days. I went banana boating and parasailing, took in a show at the aquarium, and went for a ride in the famous glass-bottomed boat. Water skiing, beautiful beaches, Eilat had it all. But there was nothing that made Eilat unique over any other waterfront city.

Finally it was time for me to get back to the Dan Panorama Hotel and get my stuff together for the race in Rosh HaNikrah.

A bus with the words "Millennium Tours" printed on its side was parked outside the Dan Panorama in Tel Aviv, and everyone was busy loading the bottom with backpacks, food, and water jugs. Our bus driver, a man in his fifties with a permanent sunburn, introduced himself as Tzvika and gave us a little speech about keeping his new bus nice and clean.

Although the actual race was going to be held at Rosh HaNikrah, we were going to stay in Tiberias the night before. We made very good time, Tzvika driving between 90 and 110 kilometers per hour the whole time, with just a small break on the way for drinks and snacks. We arrived in Tiberias three and a half hours later and checked into a hotel, a long low building with an unfinished roof and many flags hanging in front of it.

We then made our way to the dining room for lunch. The room overlooked the Kinneret and through the big bay windows I could see sailboats, rowboats, and motorboats on the lake. I itched to get back into a boat. Since this was the last race, everyone was very excited, even though there would be only two contestants, me and a boy named Jay. It was scary going down to the wire, coming full circle from our first race on the stormy English seas to the sunny, sparkling waters of the Mediterranean.

After dinner we went to the pier to check out the night life of Tiberias. It was short and sweet — about a block of stores and restaurants, arcades and slot machines, and a big neon sign that said "Disco Boats." And who was standing by that pier waiting to file onto a disco boat? Not your average crowd of teenagers. Instead I saw row upon row of boys around seventeen or eighteen years old, all with fringes hanging from their pants and wearing black velvet caps on their heads like my friends from Massada! I was very surprised. Why would religious boys be waiting to board a disco boat? I edged over to them, hoping someone would give me an explanation.

A boy with light brown hair and a baseball cap noticed me

looking at them. "What's up?" he asked in English.

"Um, I was just wondering if religious guys like you were actually going onto one of these boats," I replied.

"Oh, don't worry," he reassured me with a broad smile. "This is part of our school's end of year bash. We've rented a boat just for our group. We're going to play our own music and dance and even make a barbecue." Then I could see him thinking to himself. "Why don't you join us tonight?" he asked me.

"I really appreciate the offer," I replied, "but I'm racing early tomorrow morning and I need a good night's sleep."

The boy looked at me earnestly and grabbed my hand. "What's your name?" he asked.

"Keith," I told him.

"Keith, listen to me. If you come with us, I promise that tonight will be a night you will never forget." He took off his baseball cap, adjusted the black skullcap that had been hiding underneath, and handed the baseball cap to me. "Here, put this on. You'll feel more at ease."

What was I doing?! This was crazy; it was almost as if a force beyond my control was leading me, pushing me in a direction I wasn't sure I wanted to be pushed. But he was such a nice kid, genuinely warm in a way that not too many people are. So I went.

My newfound friend, whose name was Bentzion Gold, told me a little about his school — a yeshivah, he called it. It was for post–high school American kids who wanted to learn in Israel for a little while before starting college. I wondered what kind of learning he was talking about, and when he saw my confusion he clarified, "Studies of the Talmud."

"Sorry, Ben," I said. "I never heard of it."

He was about to explain, but there was no time because everyone was boarding the boat.

The boat gleamed with a fresh coat of white paint and was

outfitted with a nice big sound system. Right away two boys took over the system from the disc jockey, and music started blaring from the speakers. We must have been a sight as we moved away from the dock, lights blazing, strobe lights swirling. In a corner of the smaller upper level four boys had started up the barbecue and the smells of roasting burgers and franks started wafting through the boat. The rest of the gang seemed intent on earning their meal by working up a solid sweat, and dancing began on the lower deck.

The music was highly contagious and easy to dance to. I found myself being pulled into the circle by a few guys and propelled into the inner circle to dance with one of their rabbis. I think he was a rabbi because he had a big bushy beard. The dancing was like nothing I had ever seen before. My friends danced to impress people with their dancing abilities. Here nobody seemed to care if anyone was watching. They had unbridled enthusiasm as they celebrated life, and the happiness on that boat could have cheered up Oscar the Grouch! Picture the scene. The lake was pitch black, its water smooth and shiny, surrounded by mountains like spectators at a ball game. In contrast, the boat was lit up and packed with action. Tens of boys danced with terrific enthusiasm in numerous circles, faces red and flushed with effort, chests heaving.

After forty-five minutes, the music was lowered and the boys' tempo slowed. The food was ready, and we happily partook of the meal. Dancing had given me an appetite, and the water always makes me hungry, so I really packed it in. Then, from across the lake, a motorboat containing three men approached rapidly. They pulled up next to the boat and boarded. The one who stuck out the most had a long white beard and luminous eyes shining with obvious intelligence.

"Keith," whispered Bentzion, "that's our *rosh yeshivah*, the head of our school."

"Wow," I said. "He looks like an angel!"

"He's a tremendous scholar and holy man, known worldwide for his piety." He certainly looked like a sage was supposed to look. "That younger guy is one of the best singers in the religious world today," continued Bentzion, "and the third man organized this event."

The three men made their way over to the microphone and the organizer started to speak. He thanked the chaperons and the boys for giving their all to the program and then introduced the glowing faced man and invited him to speak.

I hardly understood a word he said, but his presentation was enough to make an impression on me. Just the fact that there were people around who looked like him was unbelievable. He was totally different from any reverend I'd ever seen on TV, and the boys were listening with great interest.

What kind of people were these? He finished speaking much too quickly for me. I could have looked at him all night. Suddenly Bentzion was propelling me over to him. A path cleared, and when we reached him Bentzion whispered something into the ear of the man in charge, who in turn bent down to the white-bearded man and asked him something. He beckoned me over, his hand outstretched, and spoke to me.

"They tell me you joined us tonight without planning to. That is a good sign. It shows me that Heaven is directing you along the true path without you even having a choice in the matter. Do not get sidetracked from what you perceive as the truth. When something is real, it speaks to a person's soul, and there is an instant connection, which only a truly honest person will acknowledge. Try to be that intellectually honest person." He looked at me searchingly and there was immense sadness in those beautiful eyes as he said, "There will be much hardship and pain on the road you will take. Don't let that throw you off." He took out a card on which was written his phone number and gave it to me. "If you ever need me, give me a call. I'll be available for you at all times. Don't hesitate."

Meanwhile the singer was getting himself set up at the front of the boat with his cordless mike, and the boys running the sound system slipped a disk of his musical sound tracks into the machine. This guy had a magical voice, smooth and sweet, hitting the high notes with ease. I could see that the boys idolized him and I thought how good it was that their stars were people like these rabbis. Even the singer looked like a respectable fellow.

The boys put their arms around each other's shoulders and danced slowly in a circle, singing the chorus of the song with the singer like one big happy family. I had noticed that things were much more informal here in Israel — the singer didn't seem to mind standing in the midst of the crowd. There was something appealing about this country of unbashful people, who spoke their minds and told you what they thought straight.

I was able to pick up the tune they were singing right away. I didn't follow the words, but it didn't matter, since I got the feeling, the mood, even without knowing the words. Bentzion was right. It was a night I would never forget.

It was also a night that I wouldn't have any sleep. By the time we got back to the dock it was close to three in the morning. I said good-bye to Bentzion, thanked him for an unforgettable evening, and took his phone number, promising to stay in touch.

I finally got back to my hotel at around four o'clock, but I was so keyed up I knew I wouldn't be able to fall asleep right away, so I turned on the TV. The only thing on at that hour was a documentary about Indians, but I watched it until I fell asleep at around six o'clock.

I was awakened at seven-thirty for breakfast. Talk about

groggy. I felt as if a hippo had sat down on my head, it hurt so much! But I pulled myself out of bed to the dining room and consumed a gallon of ice coffee and two Tylenols, after which I was ready to take on the world. Sleep? That was for lesser mortals. I had a race to win!

It was a warm day, so I changed into my bathing suit and put on my T-shirt with the Nike slogan, since Nike was my sponsor. I adjusted my watch, ready to show the mirror on the wall who sailed the best of all.

We took a bus to Rosh HaNikrah and arrived at the race's starting point at ten o'clock sharp, each of us finalists with a look that said, "Today I am a winner!" One big white cloud directly above us prevented the sun from shining in our eyes, and I took that as a good omen. What a day! Pleasant breeze, spiffy new sailboats, sails flopping joyfully in the wind. Two boats, one red and one white, were moored close together at the dock. I got into the white boat and prepared to cast off, after going through my checklist carefully. Everything was in order.

The boats were released and shot out into the churning sea. We nudged each other's craft, trying to get a better position to begin with. And then all of a sudden, we heard the gunshot, the signal to begin.

I moved with my boat. It was such a small craft that where I put my weight influenced how the boat moved to a great extent. I used all my sailing tricks, holding nothing back. Soon I was in the lead, my boat swiftly cutting through the waves. The further into the sea we got, the bigger the waves became. Soon they were a threatening size. We plowed through them, determined to show who was boss. I moved my sails up to their highest point and felt the influx of energy the wind was giving me. My boat and I became one. As soon as my mind decided what to do the boat understood, and it was done! We jumped the waves, rode them up, slid them down, laughing as we flew like a jet in the sky.

A giant wave came threatening to drown us, and we dodged it artfully. I stuck my tongue out in victory! Then we came to a smooth spot. The water was a little calmer, and I relaxed my grip on the wheel and spread my arms wide at the sky, reveling in the joyfulness of it all.

And then without any warning, a huge wave threw itself at my boat. With my hands spread out, I wasn't bracing myself on anything, and I was lifted off my feet and thrown up into the air.

I spun around without control over anything. As I came down in slow motion, I caught a glimpse of Jay in his boat with a look of total shock on his face.

My boat had already moved out from under me. I tried to catch the edge but missed. My head hit the side of the boat hard. And then there was only darkness.

Chapter Six

New York City

The headquarters of Salvador and Sons occupied an old but beautifully renovated and furnished building on the Manhattan waterfront. Mirrored windows reflected the sunlight right back at whoever was looking at them.

A bank of computers surrounded a guard, whose job it was to monitor the front, back, and sides of the property. Anyone who wanted to enter had to ring the bell and give his name, which was screened by the computer. If he was found to be acceptable, the doors would glide open and the guard, a scowling, hulking young man in black suit and tie, would frisk him. Only then was he permitted to continue on his way to the particular floors his business was on.

Today, a very nervous young man waited outside the steel doors. He was elegantly attired in a dark blue silk suit and a blue and gold tie. His name was Kevin, and he was there to see Mr. Salvador.

He wasn't a very happy camper, knowing as he did that the boss wasn't going to be thrilled with his news.

The buzzer sounded and the camera swung itself in his direction, giving him the once-over. He made a rude gesture at it and growled his name into the intercom. The doors slid open, and he submitted to a check by Tony, who informed him that the boss wasn't in the best of moods and he should watch his step.

This bit of news didn't make Kevin any happier, but he quickly made his way across the gleaming marble floors to the elevator bank. The pictures on the walls were all originals, all behind glass, the recessed lighting showing them off to their best advantage. A person could be forgiven for thinking this was a very respectable company.

The truth was that Salvador and Sons, while dealing in respectable trades such as real estate, construction, and imports and exports, dealt also in some very shady activities such as gambling, loan-sharking, and drug running.

The tentacles of the man in charge, Benito Salvador, spread far and wide, to many countries in the civilized and not-so-civilized world. Some knew him as the boss, but most knew him as Bulldozer Salvador.

His temper was legendary, his mood swings incredible. He was as gentle as a lamb one minute and a roaring tiger the next minute. His unpredictability was his greatest weapon. The men who worked in the same fields as Bulldozer Salvador made sure they didn't mess with anything he was involved in. It just wasn't worth it.

Kevin pressed the button for the ninth floor, where the boss's office was located, and got in when the elevator arrived. It was a noiseless ride, and Kevin was sweating despite the air conditioning throughout the building.

The door opened with a ping, and Kevin stepped out onto the thick carpeting that lined the floors. A man dressed in a black Armani suit, a shoulder holster bulging under his arm, was waiting for him.

"How are you, Kevin?" sneered Sylvester Salvador, son and

heir apparent to the Bulldozer. Harvard educated and as polished as they come, Sylvester Salvador had proved his worth many times over in his long history as the number two to the Bulldozer. "My father is waiting most impatiently for you; please come with me."

Kevin followed Sylvester down the long hallway, the thick carpet muting their footsteps. At the end of the hallway, they turned left and came to a pair of intricately carved wooden doors.

Sylvester swung open the doors without knocking, and they passed through the outer office, where a man stood up to greet them, checking Kevin yet again before Sylvester took him into the door at the far side of the room.

It was a huge penthouse suite, glass windows stretching across the length of the room in place of walls. The view of the ocean was astounding, and at the port one could see boats docking and merchandise being loaded all the time.

Beside the windows sat the Bulldozer, Benito Salvador, clad in a beige suit and an impeccably knotted cream-colored tie. Cuff links in the shape of tiny pool tables adorned his monogrammed shirt. He was smoking a cigar as he stared at the harbor. His huge, solid oak desk sat between him and Kevin.

He turned to look at Kevin, his gray eyes penetrating. The Bulldozer was smiling now; at his affable, charming best. Unfortunately, his worst rages came after such behavior.

"Have a seat, Kevin," he said, waving his cigar in the air. Kevin sat in one of the deep armchairs in front of the desk. This furniture had a purpose, of course; the boss always made sure he was higher than the person he was meeting with. "Brief me, Kevin," he said in his rumbling voice.

Kevin wished he knew where to start. He collected his thoughts, thinking back over the last few years.

Of all the people in Benito Salvador's world, there were few

he could stand, and fewer still who could stand him. One of the only mutual friendships he enjoyed was with the person whom he had been closest to in the world: his one and only daughter, Nicole.

A very attractive girl, Nicole had none of her brother's slyness, none of the family's cunning; she was a guileless person, very friendly, very vivacious, and she loved her father more than anyone in the world. The Bulldozer returned her love in spades. One of his greatest pleasures was to come home after a hard day's work and have dinner with Nicole.

Since Mrs. Salvador had died years before, the young Nicole had always been the woman of the house, hosting all the parties and appearing with her father at numerous festivities.

Six months before, the Bulldozer had arrived home and found a note from Nicole waiting in his study. In it she explained that, as much as she loved him, there was something missing in her life which she couldn't really describe; therefore, she had decided to leave home and go find whatever it was that was lacking. She would be in touch, and she didn't want him to chase after her. When she found what she was looking for she would come home. "Love, Nicole," the note ended.

The Bulldozer didn't entertain that idea for a second! Not go after her? Who did she think she was kidding? The Bulldozer had looked around his study. Brocaded drapery hung from the windows; the desk was an antique captain desk acquired at Sotheby's; his pens were gold Mont Blancs. But without Nicole it wasn't worth anything to him.

The Bulldozer quickly decided to put Kevin DeMartino on the case. Kevin was a man who could be spared from the everyday running of his organization. He was a good, dedicated worker, who was able to keep on something until he found what he was searching for.

A few years back, there had been a leak in one of their Panama cocaine routes. Police had been tipped off a few times; his men had been ambushed, and, in general, someone was opening up his mouth a wee bit too much. Whoever it was had to be put out of commission.

A group of higher members of the organization had traveled to Panama to investigate. Kevin, then younger, who had gone along as a bodyguard and had ended up finding out who the mole was, thereby securing the route.

The Bulldozer had been impressed. There was no immediate promotion for Kevin; that wasn't the way things went, but he'd been kept in mind. He'd been used again not long afterwards.

There had been some funny business going on in one of the organization's casinos in Prague. Kevin had been sent down to make the problem disappear. A few days later, the manager of the Magic Elixir, as well as the top pit boss, were found floating in the Mauldau under the Charles Bridge. Yes, Kevin had proven himself.

And now it was time for him to take on something a little more difficult: tracking down the Bulldozer's daughter and convincing her to come home.

And so Kevin had gone abroad for a couple of months. Finally he was back, and the Bulldozer sincerely hoped for good news.

Kevin cleared his throat. "I know I've sent in weekly progress reports, but I'll start from the beginning of my investigation anyway. The very first thing I did was get our man at the airport involved. After some arm twisting, he was able to inform me that Nicole had taken an Air Alitalia flight to Rome. From there she flew to Israel. My destination immediately became Israel.

"Upon arriving, I figured she hadn't come to Israel to sun at Eilat; most probably, she had gone to Jerusalem. Having been raised Catholic, Nicole probably headed to that ancient city to find a place to study and allay her doubts.

"Armed with her picture, I started checking out convents. Of course, nuns are not prone to disclosing information, but I was able to tell, from their facial expressions and body language, that they were telling the truth when they said she hadn't been there. After about three months, I ran out of places to check in Jerusalem and started going further out."

The Bulldozer listened in silence as Kevin continued his story. "I rented a car and began exploring the countryside, stopping by anything my map indicated could be religious. Finally, at an old and crumbling stone convent in the Sinai Desert, I found a nun who told me Nicole had been there for four months. She had not been satisfied with anything she heard and had gone up to Jerusalem to find — get ready for this shocker — a Jewish school to check out! Nicole told the nun when she left that perhaps, in the mother of all religions, she'd find her place!"

The Bulldozer's face had turned white with Kevin's last bit of information. This part of the story was new to him. It was obvious that he was just barely keeping himself under control.

"I turned around and went back to Jerusalem," continued Kevin, "where I started finding out the different options for someone like Nicole."

The Bulldozer's eyes, hard as chips of rock, were fixed steadily on Kevin's face. He motioned Kevin to continue. "Well, after speaking to a number of religious Jews, I found out the three or four places she might be, and I paid them a visit.

"And, finally, in one school, when I spoke to the woman in charge and showed her a picture, the look on her face gave her away and I knew I had struck gold. When I started interrogating her, she informed me that the girl in the picture had especially requested not to be discussed. Well, I simply blackmailed her — I threatened her with all sorts of things, ranging from getting the government involved to abducting Nicole until she finally gave in and arranged a meeting between us."

The Bulldozer sat motionless waiting for Kevin to continue. "I must tell you," said Kevin, looking the Bulldozer straight in the eye, "I didn't have much hope before I met her, and once she walked into the room, I knew the game was over. She was dressed very modestly in a sweater and skirt, and could've passed for any of the religious girls I'd seen in the country.

"She opened the conversation. 'I was under an illusion that my father wouldn't come after me. I was wrong. However, I want to make something very clear. There is absolutely no way I'm coming back to Manhattan with you. I've searched and searched, feeling extremely lost and confused. None of the Christian theological experts I've gone to were able to satisfy my soul's yearning for truth.

" 'So I'm here now at this school, and for the first time in my life I've heard some things about religion and belief in God that finally make sense. Tell my father I still love him; however, this is my life, and I don't want him mixing into it now.'

" 'Nicole, tell me one thing,' I said. 'Are you planning on converting to Judaism?'

" 'As of now, I still haven't decided; although it's very possible that it will come to that. Don't look so shocked, Kevin,' she told me, with a hint of her old laughter. 'It's not as bad as if I became an addict, is it?'

"I wasn't so sure, but I asked, 'Can you get in touch with your father?' She was already on her feet, moving towards the door. She turned and looked back over her shoulder and said, 'Tell my father he must forgive me for now, but I can't have a relationship with him.' Then she was gone."

Kevin finished his narrative and looked at the Bulldozer for his reaction.

The Bulldozer's gray eyes were alive with fire. He paced the room from wall to window. At last he walked back to the desk, and Kevin and Sylvester braced themselves for the explosion.

The Bulldozer slammed his fist down on the oak desk. "Jewish!" he roared. "She has no place better to go to for meaning? How could a devout girl who grew up in a church, never missing mass, give up such beauty for ancient meaningless nonsense!"

He strode to the far side of the room, overturning furniture in his wake, kicking chairs out of the way, until he reached the minibar, where he poured himself a tall glass of scotch from a crystal decanter.

"How can she do this to me?" he yelled, between gulps of scotch. A red vein stuck out on his forehead. "I am her Papa, and I have a responsibility to make sure she won't do something that she'll regret.

"Kevin, go back to Israel, with another of my boys, and keep your eyes on her. Any news you find out must be relayed to me at once! I especially must know if she's going to convert — do you understand me? If you fail in this, I won't be held responsible for what I do to you!

"Now, go," bellowed the Bulldozer. Kevin jumped up from the armchair, turned around, and made his way out of the room as the gray Manhattan sky grew more overcast and the fog closed in on the ninth floor windows.

Chapter Seven

Teveriah

A whitewashed hospital room. I'm in a big bed. Machines beeping, monitors flashing, red lights moving up and down. An IV attached to my arm. My head, it hurts so much, such a banging, pounding feeling. My vision is so blurry. What am I doing here? People standing around my bed, familiar faces — my parents, my coach, friends here to see me. I can't say hello, I can't say anything! My head hurts too much to talk. Wetness on my cheeks, on their faces also, tears? Can it be? Am I crying? I don't feel like I'm crying. Can't keep my eyes open anymore — too tired.

Gradually I was able to keep my gaze focused for a longer amount of time. Every time I looked they were still there waiting, talking to me, telling me what happened. An accident! Keith Caseman, world-famous Keith Caseman had had an accident! How could it be? Those things didn't happen to me. Apparently, my condition wasn't too bad — I had been lucky. I didn't feel lucky....

Finally my eyes started clearing, my head felt less fuzzy. The nurse took out my IV and they started feeding me. I soon understood that I had been hit on my head, and when I first arrived at the hospital, the doctors thought I had suffered serious damage. They were amazed at how rapidly I was recovering.

My parents had flown to Israel. They talked to me continuously, telling me news from back home and what had happened on the Mediterranean. I knew inside what had occurred. I had grown overconfident and done something a person should never do. I had taken my hands off the tiller in a small boat in choppy water. I had made a mistake!

What can I say? My parents, who had checked into one of the hotels in the area, would ask me about the other races, and I'd reply. They thought I was very disappointed about not winning the contest.

The truth was, winning the contest no longer seemed important to me. I didn't know what had brought about this change of heart. Maybe it was the combination of everything that had happened to me since my arrival in Israel. I didn't tell my parents that — I didn't want to scare them more than they already were. But I knew that, sooner or later, I would have to make some decision that would make a lot of people very unhappy. I wasn't sure where I was headed, but as I looked out my eighth-floor window at the lake in the distance, I knew that something had changed in my attitude.

Estelle called me on the phone from Illinois almost every day, but a certain distance had grown between us that, try as I might, wouldn't go away. She sensed it and knew inside that what she had feared was becoming a reality. My parents wanted to know when I was coming home, but I told them I didn't know. My life was suddenly full of possibilities like never before. There was a whole world that I had never discovered, and I knew it was up to me to explore the unrevealed until it became clear.

Sometimes, when no one was around, I'd get out of bed and

walk down the hall to the recreation area on my floor. Since this floor was part children's ward, the recreation area was a big playroom with lots of bright pictures on the walls — gardens of colorful flowers, the Swiss Alps, castles in far-off lands, and little babies hiding in cabbages, their fat little tummies waiting to be tickled. There were plenty of toys, little chairs and tables, a blackboard for playing school, a dollhouse, and all sorts of delightful things.

There was also a piano. That was mine. I would sit down on the small black bench, flex my fingers to take away the stiffness, and slowly open the top to uncover the gleaming black and white keys. If there were kids in the playroom, I'd play the music that they liked — clowns, chopsticks, and nursery rhymes. When I got tired of that I'd play whatever I wanted to play: Chopin, Irving Berlin, and songs of the musicals — "Singing in the Rain" and such. I'd play contemporary music, too — pop songs from the late seventies and early eighties, songs from my childhood.

My fingers would fly across the keyboard as if they had a mind of their own. The nurses loved it. At first they'd peek in at me from the nurses' station; then, when they got friendlier, they'd come in to listen and enjoy the music. The music brightened up the faces of the kids, and the whole ward became a much cheerier place while I played.

My parents were showing signs of restlessness, and they left me alone for a few days to take a tour of Tel Aviv. A few days passed without a call from Estelle. That was fine with me. I don't know why, but the connection between us had been broken. Maybe it went with the watch, which had been destroyed in the accident.

Those kids in the ward — they broke my heart. Some of them were cancer patients, their heads bald as a result of the chemotherapy. Others would wheel themselves into the playroom at the sound of the first chord and sit and listen, looking up at me with big, adoring eyes. And then there were the children who had been hurt in terrorist attacks — mutilated, scarred, not only in body but also in soul.

Music brought those children back to a sunny time in their lives, to joys that they had had. For a while they were kids again, untroubled. Coming from America, I had a hard time understanding how anyone could purposely do something to hurt these innocent, unprotected sweethearts. There was Yaakov, age seven, who would have clapped his hands to the music if they weren't all bandaged up from picking up a schoolbag that he found in his schoolyard. Then there was eleven-year-old Chaya, who was blind in one eye as a result of being on a bus that had been blown up. I loved these kids, and I played for them for hours. I would go back to my bed exhausted, but it was worth it.

The second afternoon after my parents left, a bearded man walked into the playroom while I was playing. His hands were full of equipment: wires, microphones, and a monitor. There were about twenty kids with him, wearing velvet caps on their heads. He sat and listened for a while as I played, and then he introduced himself to me. His name was Shalom Weiss, and he ran a children's choir in Safed, or Tzefas as he called it. They were here to give a show for the hospital children, which they did about once every two months.

He asked me my name. I told him. "Well, Keith," he said, "I like the way you play. Maybe you can accompany us on the piano, since all we have here with us are some sound tracks. Your playing would definitely add a lot to our performance."

"Shalom," I said, "I don't know any of your songs."

"Don't worry," he said, "you'll pick them up. We sing each song three to four times. By the third time around, I'm certain you'll be playing right along with us."

He seemed like a really nice guy, with a trimmed beard, blond hair, and brown eyes. He asked me what I was doing in the hospital. I told him the story of the race, and he sympathized with me. I helped him set up his equipment for a few minutes, but I tired quickly, and, besides, I wasn't allowed to exert myself. I settled down in front of the piano and waited to begin playing.

The choir was better than I expected. The soloists had clear sweet voices, and I got into the music quickly. After hearing each song twice, I was able to play along with ease. So I played the whole concert without knowing one song! Shalom was very happy. He came over to me at the end, beaming from ear to ear. "Keith, you're amazing! Can I make you an offer? When are you getting out of the hospital?"

"In another week," I told him. "The doctor wants to keep me under observation to make sure no permanent damage has occurred."

"Well," said Shalom, "after you leave the hospital, what do you say to coming up to Tzefas for a while and playing for me on a regular basis?"

The idea intrigued me. Although I love music and play well, I'd never invested serious effort in that direction. I promised Shalom I'd think it over. Shalom left me his phone number and we said good-bye.

Since it was late in the evening, I played one last song for the kids before they had to go and eat supper. I think it was "You Are My Sunshine." Then I closed up shop for the night.

The next day there were some new children at my afternoon show. Three kids from one family. They had been on a school trip and a terrorist had blown himself up right next to their school bus. Two of the kids were in stable condition. The other one, seven-year-old Sharon, was in pretty bad shape. When I met her, I could see from the way she watched me play that she loved to play the piano. She sat and listened, never taking her eyes off me. She was in pain the whole time, with one foot seriously injured, and shrapnel wounds all over. I looked at her fingers, and my heart lurched inside my chest.

This little girl who loved to play was missing four fingers. She saw me looking at her hand and said, "I used to play the piano, too. We have one at home. But now I can never play the piano again." No dramatics, just a stoic acceptance of God's will.

"Sharon, will you come here, please?" The nurse wheeled her over and sat her on the seat next to me, and together we played a song. I compensated for her when she needed to press keys with fingers that weren't there. The whole ward was in tears, the nurses, the kids, and most of all, me. When the song was over, she smiled at me. "Thank you," she whispered. "Thank you very much."

That became our routine for the next few days. After I'd finish my daily playing for the kids, I'd wheel Sharon over, sit her next to me on the bench, and play the piano with her. She loved our playing time. It was the highlight of her day.

And then something happened that I'll never forget as long as I live. We were playing "Puff the Magic Dragon," the last song together before she returned to her room, when Sharon suddenly slumped down and turned very white. I yelled for the nurses. They came running with all sorts of equipment and hooked her up right then and there, lying her down on the piano bench. The monitor beeped wildly as if it too was in a frenzied state of mind. Through all the commotion, Sharon's face was placid, expressionless except for a certain peacefulness. Her fingers rested lightly on the edge of the piano.

Doctors had gathered around and nurses hovered at the edge of the group, ever ready to carry out their bidding. I found myself pushed to the very edge of the group, but suddenly I caught Sharon's gaze through the crowd. She looked over at me, her eyes unfocused. Clearly she was delirious.

"It's Chanukah," she said. "We're all sitting at home around the table.... The menorah is burning on the windowsill.... We're all there, Mommy, Daddy, Michal, Ari, and me.... Savta says, 'Go play the piano for us, Sharon....' I'm playing. It feels so good."

Suddenly she went into a convulsion. As she shuddered violently she gazed around the room, as if seeing something far, far away. Her breathing sounded more shallow, her small shoulders heaving with the effort of a body drained of its strength but still trying to maintain its grip on life. Then she closed her eyes and smiled peacefully. It was over.

Two days later, Sharon's parents came to see me. I had gone to the funeral, which was held in the hospital's auditorium, but I hadn't had the opportunity to speak to them there. Her parents pressed me to tell them exactly what happened in the last moments, how she had looked and what she had spoken about. When I told them that her last words were about her family, they wept unashamedly. I described to them how she had enjoyed her music to the end and that she had passed away with her fingers on the piano keys. Her parents thanked me with tears streaming down their faces. I shook hands with Sharon's father and smiled and nodded to her mother through my tears. I wished them all the very best and then went to lie down, emotionally and physically drained.

It was all I could do not to run out of the hospital after that. Although I wasn't scheduled to leave until the next day, I met with my doctor a few hours later and begged to be released.

The doctor, Dr. Yoram Ben Shabtai, was a gaunt, middle-aged man, bald except for a monk's haircut with tufts of hair protruding over his ears. His eyes bulged out a little when he was making a point.

He said, "Keith, when you arrived we were afraid you'd suffered brain damage because you hit the boat near the top of your neck. But, thank God, you recovered extremely well, with, I'm happy to report, absolutely no permanent damage. Since you're in such a rush to leave, I'd recommend you doing just that as soon as possible." Then he wagged his finger at me. "If you suffer traumatic backlashes from the death you witnessed here in the hospital, I can suggest a psychologist who can help you."

I thanked him and said I would make sure to get involved in some sort of healing activity to ease my pain. Then I shook hands, said good-bye, and went to call my parents to come get me. After packing my stuff, I went to the playroom for one last concert. All the kids were there, and they were very upset to hear that I was leaving. I was not too happy myself, knowing how much I was going to miss them all. So I played all their favorite songs.

At four o'clock my parents came to the hospital in a taxi to pick me up. I hugged everyone good-bye and left.

We rode to the hotel where my parents were staying, and I brought my belongings up to their room. Then we went out for dinner at a quaint little place overlooking the Kinneret. My Dad ordered salmon steak and baked potatoes, Mom asked for the lox platter, and I went for a steak and fries.

"So," said my mother, opening up the conversation, "when do you want to go home? Should we book plane tickets for tomorrow morning?"

I looked around the restaurant. It was on a balcony, with plants growing all around, some snaking up the wall. I felt like getting up and diving off the balcony into the lake below rather than answering the questions.

"Actually, Mom, I was thinking of staying in Israel another couple of weeks...at least."

Mom looked at me in surprise. Even Dad raised an eyebrow. "Perhaps you haven't looked at the calendar in a while, Keith," Mom said, "but it's already the end of August. College is starting next week. What do you mean, you'd like to stay? Your races are over, and you've been here almost a month already, with the hospital stay and all."

"I know," I said, "but I think I need to spend a little more time here."

My mother's face became white. This was what I was afraid was going to happen. She turned to my father and said, "Tell him, tell him he has to come home!"

My father looked from me to my mother. "Joannie, Keith is a big boy — he can make his own decisions, just like we did when we were his age."

"In general, I agree with you," said my mother, "but it's just that Israel is such a scary place! Look at all those attacks! And all the fanatics who don't let anyone lead his life the way he wants to!"

"Mom," I interrupted heatedly, "you happen to be totally wrong on that subject! I've met some of those 'fanatics' and I found them to be great people, and a lot more real than most people I know back home."

My mother was crying now. "It might seem that way, Keith," she said. "They might look accepting; they might seem sweet and kind, but they run your life, if you let them, with all their restrictions and rules. If you want a happy life, come back with us; don't stay here!"

"Listen, just because I want to stay here awhile that doesn't mean I'll never come home, you know."

"It's a beautiful country, Keith, but people come for a year and end up staying for twenty years."

"Well," I said, "I just watched a seven-year-old girl die in the hospital. She had a brilliant future — she could have become an extremely talented musician. I played piano with her and gave her some happiness in her last days on earth. I feel like it's our job to strengthen this brave and ravished country, rather than run back to our comfortable homes and sleek cars.

"That girl died for her country; she died dreaming of a holiday called Chanukah. We never celebrated that, and we should have. It seems to me that Sharon had something in herself that most people never obtain. What do you have in mind for me? College, the autumn leaves falling on the ground, the cheerleaders, apple pie? Do me a favor, please give it up. Are we just going to a party, or will we do something important for someone else?"

My mother put her head down on her arms and cried. My father was watching me with a puzzled look on his face. He'd never seen me so passionate about anything before.

For a few minutes nobody said anything. Then I cleared my throat and said, "While I was in the hospital I was offered a job — a man who has a choir asked me to play for him. I'm going to accept!" Neither of them said a word; there was nothing left to say.

Finally, my mother looked at me. It seemed to me she was saying good-bye in a final way. "I love you, Keith," she said. "Always remember that."

Later that night, in the hotel room, I called Estelle to inform her of my plans. She didn't sound surprised, only sad. After a little pause, she asked, "The question I have, Keith, is this: do you still want my friendship or not?" The words reverberated over the wires between us.

"Estelle," I said, "I wish I could say I'm coming back with you to college and everything will be the way it was before, but the fact is that I've changed. Not so much that I've changed, as I've been changed. Since I came here, things have been happening to me continually."

"Like what?" she asked.

I told her about Carl, Massada, tefillin at dawn, the battle I had imagined, the conversation with the soldier, the boat ride with the boys. I told her about the hospital and playing for the kids, their reactions, my feelings — and finally about Sharon dying in my arms.

Estelle began to cry. "It's so sad," she finally said.

"Yes," I agreed, "but now you know why I can't possibly go back just now."

"I understand all that, Keith, but what about us?"

"My life right now is all mixed up. I can't give you an answer now, as much as I'd like to. I'm sorry."

I left my parents off at the airport with a hug and kiss for Mom and a handshake for Dad. As soon as they went past security, I went over to the row of public phones and dialed a number in Tzefas.

"Hello, Keith," Shalom Weiss said. "When are you coming up?"

Chapter Eight

Jerusalem

Nicole woke up and looked at her watch, barely visible in the dim light that filtered in through the drawn shades. It was 6:45 — time to daven, shower, and have something to eat before class. She sighed with contentment. Why shouldn't she be content, when at last her brain was receiving some rational explanations to the many questions that had bothered her?

Back at home, when she'd gone to the family's priest, Father O'Malley, the answers usually turned into speeches on the subject of belief. A person must trust in what he knows is holy, the priest always used to say, and eventually he experiences a flash, a moment of holy inspiration, which clears up all doubt. But until that happens, he must believe; he must have faith.

Nicole had wondered at his stupidity. Blind faith? In today's day and age, when every mystery was being unraveled and age-old vagaries were being cleared up daily? Could there really be no solutions to Nicole's difficulties and no reasons for her deep-seated pain? All might have remained as it was, and she might have lived another twenty years without doing anything to resolve her doubts, had not something happened to wake her up.

The Alfonses were very good friends of the family. It had always been that way. Antonio Alfonse had gone to school with the Bulldozer; and his wife, Catherine, had grown up in Sicily with Barbara Salvador. Antonio was Nicole's godfather and, after her mother's untimely death, young Nicole had spent hours and hours with Catherine, who comforted her and mourned with her at the same time.

Antonio was also one of the Bulldozer's closest business associates; a man of trust, whom some even referred to as the Bulldozer's consigliere. They had arrived in New York together at the right time and had bought up blocks and blocks of properties, hoping their value would increase.

They had. Within two years the Salvador Company (no sons then) had become a major player on the New York real estate scene. Antonio knew all the family secrets; nothing was hidden from him. All Nicole knew, however, was that the Alfonses were people she could rely on.

Nicole attended many parties at her godparents' beautiful home. It was not for nothing that Antonio and Catherine were known far and wide for their lavish and extremely enjoyable affairs.

Seven months before, on Nicole's nineteenth birthday, the Salvadors had received an invitation to a party the Alfonses were throwing that week. Nicole had purchased a gown by Donna Karon and had had her hair put up for the occasion. The Bulldozer had grumblingly gotten into his tuxedo, and they were driven by Kevin to the Alfonses' palatial mansion in upstate New York. The grounds had been aglow, blazing with the light of thousands of mini lightbulbs, strung across the hedges that lined the stone drive leading up to the house.

Catherine, in a gown by Oscar DeLa Renta, and Antonio, in

a tuxedo by Valentino, awaited their guests at the top of the stairs. Their faces glowed with pleasure at the sight of Nicole and her father. As usual, they had enjoyed themselves immensely.

The food had been excellent, the service up to par. The bartender knew how to mix any kind of drink a person might desire. Maybe that was what had caused Nicole to become a little tipsy. Her head started to pound, and Catherine had smiled in sympathy and brought her upstairs to one of the bedrooms to lie down until her father was ready to leave.

She'd lain between the cool sheets, her head throbbing, feeling queasy. All of a sudden, her rest was disturbed by the sound of loud voices from next door.

She'd looked around in puzzlement, not understanding where the voices were emanating from. After much inspection, she was able to discern the ducts of the heating system hidden in the fancy plasterwork on the wall, and she realized that the room next door was connected to this one through the heating system. Apparently when the ducts in both rooms were opened, one was able to hear from one room to the next.

Antonio was the one talking: "Did the shipment come through all right?" he asked.

The Bulldozer's low rumble answered; "I think so. After what happened in Venezuela last week, I thought the entire operation was in jeopardy."

"It might very well have come to that," said the Bulldozer, "but I sent down some of our boys to meet with the man who caused the whole mess down there in the first place. As it turned out, he was running our competition."

"Is that so," chuckled Antonio. "How surprising. How did you take care of the problem?"

"Well," answered the Bulldozer, "my men spread some rumors in the financial street about the quality of his company's stocks, based on some private inside information."

"Very effective," said Antonio appreciatively. "I'll bet that was a good start!"

"It was more than a good start, my friend," replied the Bulldozer. "My boys did so much damage to his company's reputation that the worth of his shares dropped by sixty percent. After that I heard the sad news of his suicide. He won't be bothering anybody for a long time to come!"

Nicole was straining her ears in disbelief. It sounded like someone had committed suicide because of her father and Uncle Antonio, and they were chatting about it as if they were discussing the price of a building they wanted to buy!

Her eyes opened wide as she heard her father chuckle. "Yes, Antonio, let them know down there in South America that someone who tries to cause problems for the Salvador family might end up finding it too tiresome to live."

Both men shared a laugh. If Nicole hadn't been feeling well before, now she felt positively horrible...her father, Mr. Devout, who never missed a Sunday service, who took religion so seriously, spoke about having caused a death as if he were telling Antonio an amusing story! How could he take it so casually?

She twisted and turned in the previously comfortable bed, looking around at all the gorgeous furnishings in the spacious room — the beautifully carved dresser, the built-in closets, the plush carpeting, the little night table with an old-fashioned brass telephone — all bought with money her father and Antonio had worked for, and now, she realized, killed for, all those years.

Here she was, so happy-go-lucky, Nicole Salvador, daughter of an influential man, enjoying life, dressing up and attending all sorts of parties; and all the time she'd been attendant to a terrible person!

Nicole had no doubt that, if confronted, her father would be able to explain away everything she'd heard. However, he wouldn't get the chance to justify himself. She was finished living a life of frivolous nonsense and false belief.

It was all she could do not to spit in disgust when she saw Antonio's cherubic face by the door as they were leaving later that night. She mumbled a good-bye to him and Catherine, blaming her rotten mood on too much alcohol. They laughed understandingly and bade her good night.

The next morning, after the Bulldozer had left for work, she'd packed her most important possessions, some of her clothes and the watch her mother had left her, and had gone into her father's study to write him a good-bye note.

She then drove her red Jaguar over to First National Bank, where she withdrew her savings of just over three thousand dollars. Her stocks and bonds she resolved not to touch. She then drove to a travel agent she'd never used before and paid cash for the cheapest ticket to Israel, which happened to be flying through Rome.

She had decided on Israel the night before as she lay in bed wondering where to go. She knew there were many Christian convents and seminaries in Israel, and she hoped she'd find someone to answer her questions. For a while, she had strongly considered Rome, the seat of the Catholic church, but after much consideration she realized that Rome would be the first place her father would search for her. Besides, Israel was so far away from home, a factor she hoped would make it more difficult for the Bulldozer to find her.

Without letting herself stop and think, Nicole Salvador, spoiled princess, heiress to one of the largest fortunes in New York, drove home, finished packing, called a cab, and directed him to Kennedy Airport, where she prepared to board her flight. As the doors closed and the plane began taxiing down the runway, she leaned back in her seat with a sigh of relief. For the first time in her relatively short life, Nicole was free, and hoping to find relief from the mysteries that plagued her.

The sun was high in the sky when the Air Alitalia jet came in for landing at Ben Gurion Airport. Fifteen minutes later, Nicole was descending the stairs to the tarmac, looking around her in fascination.

For someone who had just left a freezing New York winter, sunny Israel was a pleasant change. She removed her lambskin leather jacket and hung it over her arm, and with her other hand she hoisted her carry-on up onto her shoulder.

Now that she was here, she asked herself where she wanted to go. She decided to find a travel agent or someone who knew the country well who could direct her to a nice quiet convent — somewhere her father wouldn't think of looking for her.

She claimed her baggage and passed through customs with nothing to declare. Soon she found herself in a large room with fountains squirting water up in the air and lines of people waiting to greet their relatives as they arrived.

She looked around, momentarily at a loss. To her relief, she spotted a sign for car rentals and traveling information. They ought to know, she said to herself as she pushed open the heavy glass door and walked in.

"Hello," said the man behind the desk. "Can I help you?" He was casually clad in a white T-shirt and jeans, and his smile looked quite genuine.

"I hope so," said Nicole. "I'm looking for a quiet convent to go to — somewhere off the beaten track, a place not too many people, or preferably no one at all, visits. Can you recommend such a place?"

She crossed her fingers as she waited for his reply. The man took a thick blue book from his desk and started thumbing through it. He mumbled to himself under his breath as he flipped through the pages. "No, no good, too many visitors; too central, only men."

"I've got it," he suddenly shouted triumphantly, holding the book up in the air. "There is a convent in the Sinai Desert; very remote, extremely difficult to get to, with harsh discipline."

"How would I be able to get there?" asked Nicole.

"You can rent a car here and drive it down to Eilat, where you can leave it at our office. From Eilat, you could probably get a taxi to the convent."

Nicole didn't think renting a car was such a great idea, since she didn't know the country at all. She thanked the man for his time and opted for the bus to Eilat, which she caught from Tel Aviv.

Five hours later she arrived in Eilat. Starving, bone tired, and ready to drop, she checked into the first hotel she saw. She put her baggage down in her room, then quickly found the dining room to have a meal. Forty-five minutes later, after showering and brushing her teeth, she collapsed onto the bed and slept like a baby until morning.

Sand swirled around the taxi as it bumped along the desert road, somehow managing to penetrate the closed windows. Although it was only ten in the morning, it felt like a hundred degrees outside. Nicole watched the scenery flash by.

Lizards the same colors as the desert rocks raced from one hiding place to the next. The reddish mountains of Eilat faded into the distance, gradually being replaced by sandy brown hills. Green and bumpy cactus plants, their sharp leaves sticking out at all angles, were everywhere.

The road stretched ahead seemingly forever. After a while, they approached the border checkpoint. The Arab driver flashed his credentials to the bored Egyptian soldiers on the other side, and they drove on.

At last Nicole could see an old stone building perched on top of a tall hill. It looked like a Lego tower about to topple over.

The driver drove up as close as he could to the convent, and Nicole paid him, gathered up her bags, and got out. She stood there as the taxi made a U-turn and pulled off in a cloud of dust. And Nicole wondered what on earth she was doing, standing in the middle of the desert, thousands of miles from anything familiar.

The building was cool inside, at least in contrast with the outside temperature. Nicole had been welcomed into the building by a silent, black-robed nun, who motioned for Nicole to follow her. They entered a large chamber which seemed to stretch out endlessly, its alcoves on the far side of the room disappearing into the shadows.

The nun made a sudden sharp turn into a dark and forbidding passageway, which went on and on with offices and storage rooms opening up off of it. They continued walking in silence until they arrived at an office with a sign on it which read "Mother Superior." The nun turned around and left, leaving Nicole frightened and alone in front of the formidable door. She knocked quietly and heard a voice from within reply, "Enter."

The woman sitting behind the desk looked exactly like what Nicole would have imagined a Mother Superior to look like. Steel-gray hair peeked out from her black head covering. A pair of eyeglasses suspended from a chain hung around her neck.

She looked up at Nicole and smiled, her whole face creasing into a genuine look of welcome. She rose from behind her desk and graciously invited Nicole to take a seat in one of the armchairs directly facing her. "So," she said, seating herself in her hard, uncompromising armchair, "why have you come?"

Chapter Nine

Tzefas

Tzefas — what more do I have to say? For anyone who has never been there, my writing cannot do it justice. But I'll try. Imagine quiet, winding roads with every street, every building, a different architectural style and with a charm all its own. Picture the old city, its low stone homes clustered together, as if for protection. The new city full of pedestrians shopping, stores doing brisk business. The outskirts of the city, with its college, Talmudical academies, wedding halls, artists' quarter, and winding streets. The new and the old that is Tzefas.

And the people.... Walking down the streets are men with long tangled beards, clad all in white, their long clothes billowing around their legs, especially on Shabbos. Other men are dressed in black, with wide fur hats on their heads and white or black socks on their feet.

Some people wear no hats and instead wear knitted yarmulkes that cover their entire heads; others wear jeans and sweaters. Guitars abound.

But I'm getting ahead of myself. My bus pulled into the Tzefas Central Bus Station at about four in the afternoon. I had just spent most of the day on the bus, having come in from the airport, and I was hungry, tired, and desperate for a friend to talk to. Shalom was waiting for me when I got off the bus. "Keith," he said, giving me a bear hug, "so good to see you!" I could tell he meant it.

"You look shot to pieces, Keith. I'm gonna get you home and get some food into you and then it's bedtime."

It sounded good, I had to admit. Though Shalom had a car, he didn't use it much in Tzefas itself. He walked for the exercise, which worked out fine since Tzefas was not such a big place. We walked down one of the main streets past a stone staircase, which led up and off to the side and under a stone bridge, and then we turned left into the artists' quarter across from Yerushalayim Street.

Down the ramp we went into another world — a world of galleries, paintings in the windows, and the first autumn leaves decorating the walkway from the many trees growing in the area. Sculptures rose up in courtyards. Houses painted in blue were built inside other houses, with tall locked gates. Music wafted on the breeze.

We followed the little roads into an alleyway which led us to a wrought-iron fence.

"Home, sweet home," said Shalom, fishing a key out of his pocket. He unlocked the gate, and we made our way down a stone-lined path shaded by tall poplar trees. Then we entered the courtyard behind which the house was built. The courtyard held a grill, a picnic table with a blue umbrella, and a swing for two. *What a peaceful home*, I thought.

The screen door banged open, and four kids ran out — two boys and two girls. Shalom introduced me to my "new family," and we went into the house.

Standing in the kitchen, wiping her hands on a towel, was Shalom's wife, Shira. "Welcome, Keith," she said, taking off her big flowered apron. "I see the kids love you already. Come sit down at the table and have something to eat." I was overcome by her warmth. "Here," she said, handing me a big steaming plateful of lasagna. "Enjoy. I made it especially for you after Shalom said you were coming into Tzefas today."

I looked around as I was eating. The house opened up into the living-dining room area, which was separated from the kitchen by only a counter, no wall. A short flight of stairs led off to the other levels of the house. The red-and-white checked tablecloth, the pictures of pizzas coming out of the oven on the walls, and the kids, running, jumping, and playing all over the place, had a very calming effect on me.

I turned to Shalom. "Thank you for having me, Shalom. Do you have time for a serious talk soon?"

Shalom looked at me, his eyes shining with understanding and friendship. "I'm waiting, Keith."

I finished my meal, and Shalom asked his wife to tell anyone who called that he was busy. Then he led me into the next room, a den with comfortable if slightly worn armchairs you could sink into. A rug, toys scattered all around, and a big wooden table covered with books completed the decor. The house was built on several levels; off to the side there was another staircase leading to more rooms, some down, some up. Shalom and I sat down in the armchairs. I leaned my head on my hand and looked at Shalom. He waited for me to start talking.

"Have you ever had your whole life turned upside down in just one week?" I asked him. "Two weeks ago, I was Keith Caseman, world champion sailor. The next thing I know, I lose my race, I decide not to go to college, my parents are angry at me, and I'm about to start a whole new life in Tzefas! Talk about a 360-degree turn. Who am I now? Why did I give up my life?"

"Well," said Shalom, "first of all, who says that you must give up your whole life just like that? You could still practice boating on the Mediterranean —just rent a boat. As to going to college, you can surely go next semester. Your parents still love you. Of course, they're worried about the effect living in Israel will have on you. When you call them and you sound like your normal self, hopefully their fears will disintegrate and your relationship will go back to what it once was. Just remember: no one, least of all me, expects you to change overnight into something you're not. Hold on to your personality and if, by some chance, changes occur, that will be with your full desire."

Put like this, it didn't seem so bad.

"Now, Keith, what say to a good night's sleep?"

"Shalom, I could sleep on the swing outside and not know it tonight!"

He laughed and led me up the split level staircase to a room with a narrow bed, small built-in shower, and an exercise bike, showed me where the towels were kept, opened some drawers in the dresser, and told me he'd wake me around eight o'clock the next morning. I thanked him for everything and he shut the door.

I changed into my pajamas and was asleep before I knew it, dreaming of moonlight boat rides and men with long white beards and beautiful luminous eyes.

Shalom woke me up at 8:05 the next morning. I stretched comfortably in the big bed and then got up, showered, dressed, and went down for breakfast. Shira and the kids were not around. Shalom made me breakfast. I saw a velvet case like the boys at Massada had had for their black boxes on one of the shelves, and I thought maybe I'd put the boxes on a little later.

We spent an enjoyable hour together over breakfast, and Shalom outlined our schedule to me. First we'd go down to the place Shalom used for practice and he'd play his songs for me so I could learn them well. In the afternoon there'd be choir prac-

tice and I would join them. There was going to be a concert in Petach Tikvah soon, and Shalom wanted me to accompany them at the concert. Until now, he explained, he'd taught his choir boys songs on his guitar, but he felt that the piano was a better instrument for teaching songs.

We walked over to the small hall he used. I was very excited to see the grand piano at the far wall. I spent the whole morning learning the choir's songs. In the afternoon, at around three o'clock, the kids started to arrive. Shalom introduced me as their new piano player. We practiced together for about an hour and fifteen minutes.

After that Shalom and I packed up the equipment we'd been using and walked back to his house. The afternoon sun shone on our backs as we sauntered along one of the cobblestoned roads. I noticed an abundance of little synagogues along our route. Some were open and men stood in the doorway, calling, "*Minchah, minchah.*" I asked Shalom what that was and he explained to me that Jews pray three times a day — a morning prayer called *shacharis*, and afternoon prayer called *minchah*, and a night prayer called *maariv.*

Soon we reached a square where the street we were on met with four others. The square was paved with interesting designs and lined with benches for people to sit on. We turned left, walked down a flight of stairs, and then made a right into a courtyard with an old, old synagogue. We entered the synagogue, and Shalom gave me an English prayer book to look at while he prayed. I leafed through the pages. "Our father, our king, have mercy on us." "Blessed are You, our God, God of our forefathers...." Was He "our father, our king"?

We discussed this together after we left the little synagogue, or *beit knesset* as Shalom called it, and walked home. We passed a fish restaurant with a garden that had a sculpture in it and entered a supermarket to buy some bread and soda. One thing I had noticed about Israel — there was always some good fresh bread around.

Finally we got home, and as we entered I could see the courtyard was bursting with activity. The picnic table had been moved to the middle of the garden. There were plastic chairs set up around the table, and the grill was lit and smoking. Shira was busy laying steaks, burgers, and pieces of chicken onto the grill. The two little girls I'd met yesterday, three-year-old Avigail and five-year-old Huvi, were sitting on the swing, singing a song and swinging merrily.

The boys, six-year-old Yanky and eight-year-old Eli, were on cat patrol, bearing Super Soakers in case any feline creature with nefarious ideas in mind got too close to the grill. Anyone who dared to approach would immediately be met by a stream of cold water that would lead him to abandon his idea very quickly. Soon I was roped into mixing potato salad and coleslaw, and I even showed Shalom how to make a salad dressing he'd never seen before that my mother would make when we had family barbecues.

Shalom shlepped the stereo out of the living room onto the patio and hooked it up with an extension chord. Soon we were grooving along with something called Diaspora. We spread a plastic tablecloth on the picnic table and started putting salads and drinks out. Suddenly, there was a knock on the gate followed by a "Yo, Shalom, open up."

I went to open the gate, letting in three guys in various types of dress. One wore a big white garment over his white shirt with fringes hanging off the bottom of it. I looked down, expecting black pants. Nothing doing; he had on bright green pants. The second guy wore a T-shirt, shorts, and a big white skullcap with some sort of Hebrew slogan on it. The third wore a suit and hat, and there were blue threads mixed with the white ones hanging from his shirt. I was beginning to see that here in

Tzefas there was no such thing as a dress code; everyone had his own style, and that was fine. Two of them had guitars and, after greeting Shalom, Shira, and the four kids, they proceeded to sit themselves down at the table and start to strum together.

Shalom introduced them as boys from the yeshivah in Tzefas and told me their names. Soon, everything was ready and we all went in to wash our hands (Shalom had to teach me how). Then we all had a terrific barbecue. The guys told some stories, Shalom gave a small religious talk, and I leaned back and watched the scene.

The courtyard was bathed in soft light, the kids were swinging peacefully off to the side, and the best friends I could ask for were sitting with me. I wondered what was in store for me next! If my mother could have seen how comfortable I was at that moment, she would have lost all hope of my ever coming back....

We cleaned up quickly and sang a song or two before the guys had to go. So ended my first full day in the ancient, Kabbalistic city of Tzefas.

Chapter Ten

The week passed quickly. We worked on music a lot and Shalom loaned me his car when I wanted to tour the area. I also decided that since I was there and Shalom's black boxes were also there, I might as well strap myself up with them in the morning. Shalom helped me and cautioned me to take one step at a time. One of the afternoons, I hiked from the bottom of Tzefas to Meron, which is around two miles away. It took me about seven hours and I got back to the house dirty, scratched, starving, and happy.

On Friday, instead of going to play music, Shalom asked me to help him get ready. "For what?" I asked.

"You'll see," he answered. So I helped him wash floors, using a stick and a damp rag, and he vacuumed while I dusted. Then we changed some linen and cleaned the patio. The kids cleaned up all the toys and took baths while Shira hustled around the kitchen all day, making trays and pots of delightful looking creations magically appear, to be replaced, just as magically, by other trays and pots.

Finally, we took a break. Shalom called it a kugel break, and each of us had a huge piece of something called potato kugel, which was hot and steaming, straight from the oven. Then Sha-

lom packed some towels into a bag for us and told me we were going to the *mikveh*.

"The what?"

"The *mikveh*, Keith; we go there before the Sabbath to purify ourselves."

"How does it work?"

"So many questions. You'll find out everything in good time."

We left the house and soon began a trek down a steep hill, using a thin rocky path that curved between the stones. After descending for fifteen minutes, we were in a cemetery.

Men were streaming from all directions to a small stone building which I figured was the *mikveh*, whatever that was! We entered the *mikveh*, and I saw stairs leading down to water at the end of the room. I watched what everyone else did, hung up my clothes on a hook, and went down into the water — an ice-cold mountain stream! I lost my breath, but I went down anyhow. I felt as if I was stripping an outer layer of impurity from my body. Incredible! Purification!

Again and again I went under, reluctant to let go of the experience, until the line of people waiting to go in forced me to move out. Who would have guessed that dipping into a pit of freezing water would have such an effect! Shalom explained to me that the *mikveh* we'd just gone to was called the Arizal's *mikveh*, and it was world famous. I definitely understood why.

We climbed back up the hill, our damp towels slung across our shoulders, hair still wet. A cool wind blew across my face, stinging it. We entered the house and found it spotless, everything in its proper place. All the books that were usually out on the dining room table were gone, put back on the shelves. Six silver candlesticks were set up on a silver tray on the end of the table, on top of the sparkling white tablecloth.

The stereo was playing someone with a raspy voice who was

telling a story about Shabbos while strumming on a guitar. After a while, he began singing, "The whole world is waiting to sing the song of Shabbos!" The atmosphere was a mix of final rush and the promise of what was to come.

My first Shabbos. Shalom, Eli, Yanky, and I made our way down the little cobblestoned paths, between buildings, as the sounds of prayer started to float out from the windows. Groups of boys with hats and suits made their way through the streets to their synagogues; women in head scarves with baby carriages sat and chatted together in the square.

We reached the *beit knesset*. The leader of the prayers had a sweet, warm voice, which carried to the far reaches of the room. In the middle of what the English siddur called "Accepting the Sabbath" there was a prayer called "Come, My Beloved." The congregation reacted to it as if lit with an electric current. They rocked with it. The men picked up their faces to heaven with inspiration and song. They glowed with the Sabbath spirit. One guy in the corner with a long orange beard was dancing by himself. You want joy? These people have joy!

As the song neared its ending, the place went wild. The people formed a circle, their feet kicking up the dust, their hands clapping. The song escalated into another song with two words, "*Shabbos kodesh*," which Shalom told me means "holy Sabbath." Over and over, they sang this song. A high, that's what it was! A spiritual high.

Shalom pulled me into the circle. "Lose your inhibitions here," he said. "Let the real you come out and be expressed!"

We danced for about ten minutes straight, until finally the leader continued the prayers. When they were finished, we wished everyone else "good Shabbos" and made our way, still in elated moods, back to Shalom's house. Entering the courtyard, we could see the candles burning through the window.

The spirit of Shabbos was in the home. Shira was sitting on

the couch with the girls, praying together. They all wished us "good Shabbos," and, after a little preparation, we were ready to sit down at the dining room table and start the meal. A few yeshivah guys joined us for the meal. We sang two songs, one for the angels and one about the virtue of the Jewish woman. The family seemed different from the way they were during the week. The food was excellent, the singing delightful, and this came every week! This had to be the right way to live. Man, woman, both happy in their respective roles, secure in the knowledge that they were doing God's will. Shira was relaxed after a day of rushing. The kids were at first active participants, but then each one dropped off to sleep on the couch or the rug.

Shira brought out cakes and ice cream, and tea for those who wanted. One of the boys, a guy named Yaakov, wanted a beer, so Shira brought out some beer. What a family! So easygoing and full of fun. The boys sang, Shalom harmonizing. I took it all in. At around eleven o'clock, we said Grace after Meals. The boys said they were going for a walk and invited me to come; I accepted. Shira showed me where the key was kept outside the house and then locked the door.

It was a cool Friday night. Crickets chirped in the brush and twigs crackled under our feet as we walked in the darkness around the bends and curves of the artists' quarter. We passed the Rimon Inn and continued on our stroll. Every so often a cat would startle us by darting out from the side of the path on its way to a garbage pail or a social visit. One cat decided to follow us around and kept at a fairly close distance. One of the guys, a boy named Sruly, decided that this cat had done something wrong to him in a previous life and was following him in the hopes that he'd forgive him. "All is forgiven," said Sruly, hand over heart. Apparently, the cat wasn't impressed; he just continued on his mission.

After a while we sat down on a bench under a tree on the

side of the road. In the sky you could see what looked like millions of stars, twinkling in the distance. "Keith, I don't know what you know about Tzefas," Yaakov said, "but this is one of the most mystical cities in Eretz Yisrael. The Arizal and his students, Kabbalists of the highest degree, walked these very roads. The song you heard tonight, 'Come, My Beloved,' was written here in Tzefas. For generations, the Jews with the loftiest spirits made it their goals to live here. And," he continued, "the mysticism still lives on!"

We looked at him in amazement; he stared back. "I'm serious! I have to tell you guys a story that happened to me recently — to me and one of Tzefas's holy men." Sitting under the tree with a street lamp nearby illuminating the scene, Yaakov told his story.

He was staying in Canaan, which is a neighborhood above the Old City of Tzefas, with nine other guys who had all come to spend Shabbos in the area. On Friday night they ate at someone's house and then went for a walk around Tzefas. It had been Yaakov's first time in the city and he wanted to get a feel for its heritage, particularly its shuls. So, while his friends walked the streets, Yaakov went into an old shul and started learning.

The shul, being Sephardic, had seats going all around the wall, and Yaakov sat down in one of them. The light was arranged in such a way that he couldn't be seen easily. By two o'clock in the morning, Yaakov knew he had to leave soon and go to sleep. Suddenly, the door in the back of the shul opened, and in walked a man straight out of history. Clad in a white garment from top to bottom, with a hood on top of his head and a white beard, the man was the picture of holiness. He didn't see Yaakov as he walked to the front of the shul, all the way up to the *aron kodesh*, the holy ark. He opened the curtain, reached in, and opened up one of the Torah scrolls, which, according to Sephardic custom, stood up in the ark.

Yaakov watched as the man started reading passages from the scroll; seemingly at random, he moved the scroll to a different part and said other passages with tremendous devotion. This went on for fifteen minutes, and Yaakov watched the whole thing in fascination. Finally, the man finished what he was doing, closed up the ark, and turned around to leave. As he started out of the shul, he noticed Yaakov sitting on the side, and their eyes met.

"I looked into his eyes," Yaakov continued, "and I felt a spark pass between us, as if he was looking straight into my soul." Yaakov looked straight into my eyes, and somehow I felt the same spark that he'd felt connect with me, too, causing shivers to run down my spine. "After he left," continued Yaakov, "I went back and told the guys what happened; they laughed and told me not to take it seriously. 'Another joker,' they said, but I wasn't so sure.

"The next morning, we davened early, made Kiddush, and left Canaan to go down to our morning meal in the Old City. Walking along the street Shabbos morning, with that special feeling in the air, I told myself the whole thing meant nothing.... Suddenly, there he was in his long, white garment, floating down the street, feet seemingly not touching the ground.

"He was going from doorway to doorway and kissing every mezuzah he came to." I'd already learned that a mezuzah was the little scroll attached to every doorway in a religious home. "Whatever he was doing, I wanted a part in it. I walked behind him, kissing each mezuzah after him.

"Well," he laughed, "the other nine boys decided that if I was doing it, and this man was doing it, they might as well! You can imagine! One man in white walking down the street kissing mezuzos, and ten boys behind him doing the same. It wasn't long before people on the street were pointing and laughing. The man understood something was going on. He turned around and saw us all behind him, and again his eyes met mine and I felt that same feeling. Confused and ashamed, I said to myself, 'The next time I see this man, I must talk to him.' "

Maybe it was the silence of the night or the eerie shadows on the crumbling stone wall next to where we were sitting, but I understood exactly how Yaakov had felt.

"Sunday morning," continued Yaakov, "we all went down to the cemetery to pray at the graves. I had something very important to pray for — my mother was in her ninth month at the time and there were complications. So I was in a very serious frame of mind. We entered the old cemetery and went over to the graves, but before I started davening, I saw him! In his white cloak, he would stand out anywhere, especially in the cemetery. He is sitting next to a tombstone praying his heart out, and I walked up to him, my hand outstretched. Before I could say a word, he jumped up.

" 'Your mother is not well,' he told me, urgency in his voice. 'She's in the hospital right now! You must pray for her.'

" 'What shall I say?'

"The man gave me a list of psalms."

Yaakov leaned back and looked at us. "I never said *Tehillim* with as much emotion. When I finished, I came back to him; he stuck his hand out to me and said, '*Mazal tov*, your mother just had a boy; she and the baby are both healthy and well.' I looked at him in wonder; how did a man in Tzefas know what was going on with a woman in America! I thanked him profusely and tried to give him some money, but he refused very insistently."

I stared at Yaakov in amazement. This was turning out to be one crazy story!

"We left the cemetery and walked to the nearest pay phone. I called my home in America. My father picked up. 'Hello! *Mazal tov*!' I shouted. 'How's Mommy?'

" '*Baruch Hashem*, she's fine, but how did you find out so fast?' he asked.

"I told him the whole story. He was amazed. 'Go back and find out his name, so we can send a donation to his shul or yeshivah,' he said.

"We went back, but there was no sign of any white-robed man in the cemetery at all.

"When I tell you mysticism is alive and well here," finished Yaakov, "you can believe me!"

"Let me tell you about something that happened to a friend of mine," Avi, one of the other boys, said. "My friend, Baruch, was sick from the time he was eleven. For six years he got weaker and weaker. With time the doctors told his parents he had only months to live. Hearing that, his father decided to take him to Eretz Yisrael before he died. They toured the country and finally came to Tzefas.

"Baruch strolled around exploring the cemetery while his father went to the Arizal's *mikveh*. He saw a cave and decided to go in and explore. Inside the cave, there were a table and chairs, pots and pans hanging from the walls, and a bottle and cup on the table.

"From the back of the cave emerged an old man with a long white beard. He looked at Baruch and said, 'What is the matter with you, my son?'

"Baruch told him about his illness. The old man picked up the bottle and poured some of the contents into a cup. 'Drink,' he commanded.

" 'I'm not allowed to,' said Baruch.

" 'Please, you must, this will cure you.'

"Baruch drank it, hoping it wouldn't make his illness worse. When he finished, the old man took the cup, pinched his cheek, and told him to make sure to drink a half cup of lemon juice every day. Then he gave him a blessing.

"Baruch left the cave and saw his father waiting outside the Arizal's *mikveh* for him. He ran to him, yelling, 'Abba, come quickly; I want you to see the most amazing old man I've just met.' Together they rushed across the graveyard to the cave, climbed the stairs, ran inside, and...nothing! No table and chairs, no pots and pans, no bottle of wine, and most importantly, no old man! Baruch couldn't get over it.

"When they got back home, the doctor checked him out and, wonder of wonders, his sickness was all gone! Of course, he took his lemon juice!"

The time flew by with stories like these, and it was very late by the time I got back home. I thought about the mystical essence of this city as I got into bed, and I wondered for the thousandth time where I was going.

Chapter Eleven

New Jersey

Leaving me aside for a while, let me tell you about Zack. Why Zack? Because Zack had a tremendous influence on me, more than almost anyone else did. A lot of who I am today is because of Zack. When I was getting used to life in Tzefas, working with the choir, doing concerts, hiking, even learning here and there with Shalom, Zack was in America in *beis midrash*.

Let me take you to the scene: a dorm room like any of the dorm rooms that are located in any of the yeshivos off the New Jersey Turnpike. Some scratched furniture, an old weatherbeaten desk, three beds. The wall was graced with some posters of Jewish music events and a big sign that said "Try Brisk! Ice Tea," to which some *bachur*, in a moment of humor, had added "to get into" between "Try" and "Brisk," so now it read: "Try to get into Brisk" and in small letters, "Ice Tea."

Zack often wondered if the previous inhabitant of the room had in fact breached those heavily guarded doors and managed to get into Brisk or not. Right now, Zack wasn't doing so much wondering. In fact, right now he was pondering how unjust it all was as he dumped his drawers of stuff into a big plastic garbage bag.

Why, thought Zack to himself, does a *bachur* bother to *shteig* in *lernen* like this, to *chop p'shat* in the *rosh yeshivah*'s *shiur* all these years if, when he's finally starting to really get it, the *rosh* tells him it's time to leave? Zack sat down on the rusty old chair, scraping it back, and thought back over the past five years. He remembered coming to this yeshivah back in tenth grade, a short, awkward boy who wasn't cool by any stretch of the imagination. Most of the guys took one look at the newcomer and decided that he wasn't their type. He had ended up a loner for most of his first year at the yeshivah.

He smiled, thinking back to the many hours of hard learning he'd put in to really get *p'shat*. Slowly, things had changed. By eleventh grade, guys were already asking to be his *chavrusa*, and he had the pick of the pack. Personality took a little longer to change, but by the middle of eleventh, jokes were coming to him more quickly and he was much more at ease with himself. Zecharia became Zack, as good as nicknames went in a world where a nickname was a sign of status.

He changed in other ways, too. The short, gangly boy with big glasses developed into a tall, muscular young man, yarmulke perched sideways on his head, contact lenses replacing the glasses. By twelfth grade, he was a leader and guys were proud to call him their friend. In learning, he'd long ago caught up to the other boys in his *shiur*, and by now he outstripped them in depth by far. Through it all, he remained somewhat aloof from the other boys, although he didn't really know why. Maybe it had to do with the cold treatment he'd gotten when he'd first arrived. All he knew was that he made sure to give a warm welcome to every new *bachur* who entered the yeshivah.

Zack thought about all the phases the boys had gone through. There was the phase when Carlebach tapes were played nonstop for three months. The time when the local coffee manufacturer was giving out mini-coffeemakers as a promotion, and every room in the dorm had one. In the morning after *shacharis*, the place smelled like a coffee factory. With all this, the guys became like family, the *rosh yeshivah* like a father. For a boy who wasn't close to his real family that helped a lot. Stuck as they were, away from everything happening out in the world, life in yeshivah took on a lot more meaning.

When it snowed, which happened quite often, the snowball fights were legendary. Zack leaned back in the chair, scratching his head, a habit he had acquired back in twelfth grade, and thought about all the hours of counseling he'd given to the younger guys, who would seek him out when they came to the yeshivah. That was besides the help in learning, which he'd given to anyone who asked. He dressed well — he wasn't obsessed about it like the guys who made sure to go to every Simms bash and Saks Fifth Ave sale, but he did starch his shirts and liked everything to be neat and pressed.

He remembered the big question going around. Do guys get their shirts dry-cleaned so the pocket should stay closed, or not? Many held the reason was the pocket. If so, the reasoning continued, then if someone opened up his friend's pocket on the first day that he wore the shirt, he should have to pay the amount it cost to dry-clean it again. Zack smiled in recollection. When the *menahel* heard about this, he'd go around the *beis midrash* schmoozing with the *oilam* in learning, and during the course of each conversation he'd happen to put his finger into the guy's shirt pocket and pull as if not knowing what he was doing. The looks on their faces as the *menahel* pulled apart the starch still sent him into hysterics.

There were the funny moments and the serious times, like the *rosh yeshivah*'s Tishah B'Av *schmuess*, which he gave annually after the reading of *Eichah*. Guys who had left the yeshivah long before would come from far away to hear this talk. The *rosh* was a very informed man when it came to current events and he'd get into stride, telling the boys just how many anti-Semitic incidents had occurred recently in every country.

Once he had them in the right frame of mind, he'd launch into a burning *mussar schmuess*, scathingly direct, right on the mark. His point — are we any better than the goyim? We can learn more easily than any generation since who knows how long and, instead of doing so, we waste our time on *shtuss*! Here he'd go into a list of all the current crazes going on in the yeshivah.... Cigarettes and cell phones were very high on his hit list, as were taking trips to Shoprite and making barbecues at three o'clock in the morning.

Finally, when everyone was feeling like a *ben Torah* wanna-be, he'd move into the *churban*. With *midrashim*, stories, and the words of Chazal on his fingertips, he made life in Yerushalayim come alive, describing the service in the Beis HaMikdash until everyone sitting in the *beis midrash* could almost smell the incense burning, hear the Levi'im sing, and see the streams of people bringing trays of fruit up to Yerushalayim. And then the destruction. He'd spare no details, hitting them harder and harder until the men would become children and the tears would emerge. Tears for the destruction, but more so tears for the rebuilding. And he'd end on a soft note, expressing his fervent wish that Mashiach should come in our days.

The *beis midrash*, too, held good memories for Zack. It was where he'd developed one of his most enjoyable pastimes, namely, sitting with a *sefer* of Reb Chaim, a bag of Herr's barbecued potato chips, and a cup of strong coffee. He'd grapple with the ideas, exploring all directions. The clearly written Reb Naftali, the concise and sharp Reb Shimon Shkop, the thrill of Reb Baruch Ber's Torah, not knowing if you'd get to see the light at the end of the tunnel. And when you were able to fully grasp something, then you had the pleasure of knowing what you were doing was real and right. You just felt it inside yourself.

In his spare time he listened to music, and he was able to

name just about every song on any Jewish tape, who composed it, arranged it, sang it, and produced it. With it all, he chose his friends carefully; not just anybody who tried made it. Of course, he treated everyone nicely and with respect; he was a *ben Torah*! But true friends, thought Zack to himself, were few. There weren't many boys whom he trusted, whom he could tell his secrets to.

But, looking at the current picture, his years in the yeshivah had been happy and productive, years of growth.

He remembered his roommates fondly. First Lazar, who snored so loudly the flimsy walls shook, and when he was awakened by indignant *bachurim*, he would exclaim, "Me? I never snored in my life!" Then there was Moshe Chaim who would sneak down to the kitchen every Friday night and take all the meat out of the *cholent* for his midnight snacks. The boys were up in arms about that, but what could you do except for a *cholent* patrol? Besides, no one really wanted to get Moshe Chaim upset; if they did, he might raise the price of the Snapple he sold from one dollar to two to get even.

Then there was the year of the Goodman brothers. Zevy and Levy were the biggest characters the yeshivah had ever seen. Zevy taught himself to play harmonica, practicing until 2:00 every night. Levy taught himself to ride the unicycle. Zevy made cream cheese by filling a sock with regular cheese and hanging it out the window. Levy decided to make wine, and the next day fifty pounds of grapes were delivered to his dorm room. Levy and Zevy squashed the grapes with Schlock Rock as their background music, and the room smelled like cheese, socks, and wine for weeks. Finally they got into learning and turned their competitiveness in that direction, keeping the lights on in the *beis midrash* long after everyone else had turned in.

There was Shua the baseball fanatic, Aharon the *baal mussar*,

Simcha the *masmid*, Naftali the *leitz*, and Tzvi, who felt that a person could only acquire *gadlus* if he acquired it at two in the morning while leaning over a *shtender* with a Reb Chaim and smoking. All these Zack remembered with a fond smile.

But now it was all over, because yesterday the *rosh* had called him into his office and said, "I'm proud of the way you turned out, Zecharia, but now it's time you moved on."

At first he thought he hadn't heard correctly. The *rosh* telling him to leave? He was the best boy in the yeshivah!

But the *rosh* explained that he'd done very well and now, in order to grow further, he needed a new atmosphere. "And I know just the place; by my friend in Yerushalayim, Reb Shaya Borenstein. His *derech* in learning will give you something which mine didn't. Plus, he loves a good *shtikel* Maharal, which I know you love, too. His *Chumash shiurim* are in a class of their own, and he's truly a *chushever Yid*. I'd feel good knowing you were learning by Reb Shaya."

What could Zack say? When put like that, there really wasn't much choice in the matter, and that was why he was busy emptying out five years' worth of stuff into his suitcase, his duffel bag, and a garbage bag. He pulled the last drawer out, but it had been a tough customer from day one in this room, and always got stuck.

Now, however, with his emotions all *fartumult*, he didn't have the patience to play games with it. He gave it a good yank and two ties, three cuff link cases, a pack of cigarettes a year old, a little package of mayonnaise, a CD carrier, *The Maggid Speaks*, and his *Kovetz Shiurim* fell on the floor. Suddenly, it was too much for the best boy in yeshivah, and, with no real friend to pour his heart out to, Zecharia Zack Bernstein put his head on his arms and cried for the first time in seven years.

Chapter Twelve

Sinai Desert

It had been two months already and Nicole was no closer to happiness than she had been when she first arrived at the convent. The confusion within her, the sadness that was her constant companion, seemed to have no resolution. As the frustration slowly grew inside her like lava in a volcano, she decided to leave the convent for a few days and go air out her mind.

She informed the Mother Superior of her decision, expecting to be subjected to a deluge of criticism, but surprisingly enough the Mother Superior had only smiled and told her to do what she felt was right. A taxi picked her up and drove her to Eilat, where she checked into the Queen of Sheba Hotel, one of the most beautiful hotels in Eilat. The fact that it was expensive didn't matter to Nicole. After all, she had always lived a life of luxury.

After settling into her room, she felt hungry and remembered seeing a sign in the hotel lobby about a sushi bar on the twelfth floor. She took the elevator up to the twelfth floor and entered a very high class establishment with elegantly carved wooden tables, heavily cushioned chairs, and excellent quality linen napkins. Scanning the room, her gaze fell on the glass balcony doors.

Hesitantly she weaved her way through the crowded restaurant to the doors, which opened easily. Nicole was amazed at the view below. She was able to see eateries, a mini–amusement park, a splendid view of the ocean, and the magnificent three-section pool situated in the hotel's stunning gardens. Reentering the restaurant, Nicole asked a waitress if she could be served right on the balcony. Within a minute, a table had been set up for her and she was perusing a menu.

She had just begun her meal when the doors opened and a female soldier walked through them. She was closely followed by another waitress who proceeded to set up a second table for her, quite near Nicole's own table. The soldier slipped off her gun and sat down in silence, as she too contemplated the awesome sight before her.

Nicole tried hard to enjoy the food as she ate, but her spirits were pretty low. Her mind took her back against her will to her unsatisfying life at the convent. She didn't know what to do! The convent had seemed the perfect place for someone like her...someone with her problem. If only she wasn't constantly being plagued by doubts! She wanted to believe so much, but she wasn't going to compromise and give in if her soul still felt cheated. Oh, what should she do? She sighed deeply, feeling as if the weight of the world was resting on her fragile shoulders.

Before she knew it, she was crying in despair, her shoulders heaving as the sobs wracked her body. A shadow suddenly loomed up over her, covering her table with its elongated shape. The soldier stood there with a concerned look on her girlish face. "I'm truly sorry to intrude," she began in broken English, "but is there anything I can do to make you feel better?"

Nicole, who would normally never share her personal life story with a total stranger, suddenly felt a need to unburden herself to someone. And so, on a balcony overlooking Eilat, as the sun began its descent and the lights on the promenade far below were turning on, Nicole shared her fascinating story with the other girl.

She told of her childhood, her questions about God's will, her unvoiced aversion to her religion, and the pat answers she had always been given. She related how she had overheard the conversation which had pushed her over the brink and given her the impetus to leave. She spoke of arriving in Israel and finding a convent and of her dashed hopes of finding answers there. The soldier listened to all of this in silence, and by the time Nicole had finished her monologue, only her profile was visible in the darkness. Nicole waited to see what she would say.

The girl turned to her and said, "Why don't you leave your present surroundings and go to a different type of school?"

"Like what?" asked Nicole.

"Maybe a Jewish school," said the soldier. "I'm not religious myself, but maybe in the 'mother of all religions' you'll find your place!"

Those words entered deep into Nicole's consciousness, from where they would emerge at a later time. She smiled at the soldier through the darkness and thanked her for her concern, but she knew that she still had unfinished business at the convent. A monumental change like the one this girl was suggesting, said Nicole to herself, could only become a reality after she had exhausted all possibilities in her present situation.

A week later, Nicole, no calmer than she had been before she had left, checked out of the Queen of Sheba and returned to the convent.

Tzefas

My life in Tzefas was full, rewarding, and enjoyable. The longer I was around Shalom, the more Jewish I felt, even without him trying to convince me. Just by being himself, he was able to instill in me ideas of what life is all about. His marriage was exemplary; his talks on character improvement gave me much to think about. Slowly but surely, I found myself leaving the black boxes on for longer periods of time and saying more of the prayers in English.

I quickly became familiar with the concept of a *baal teshuvah* (one who returns to Judaism); how could I not? Tzefas was full of *baalei teshuvah*. I loved what I was doing with the choir music, but the longer I hung around the more I felt that I should be doing more in the way of religion. I started pestering Shalom for more things to observe. I got one of the boys to teach me the *alef beis*, and after a few months, with much practice, I was able to read the davening slowly by myself.

Shalom and Shira were truly delighted with this turn of events, but they were the last people to push anyone too fast. So I started to push myself. I began reading books I found — about Shabbos, Torah, the history of our people — whatever I could get my hands on, I devoured. The English *Mei'am Loez* fascinated me. Shalom was always there to make sure I didn't exhaust my energy, and he was able to answer any questions I had on what I was reading.

I got into *Nach* and Shalom brought me some ArtScroll books on the subject. *Sefer Shmuel* spoke to me, especially with all the explanations on the bottom. The more I learned, the less time I seemed to have, and soon I was being pulled in two directions at once. On one hand, I really enjoyed playing music and performing with the kids, especially when we did concerts. On the other hand, I felt that I didn't know anything and I had to go learn. Finally, I decided the time had come for me to find myself a yeshivah and settle down to some serious learning without disturbances.

I sat down with Shalom and explained how I felt — it was

time to move on. He smiled his gentle smile and said he'd help me find a yeshivah that was suitable for me. We spent a lot of time over the next two weeks checking out different yeshivos until finally we found a place that spoke to me.

It was in Jerusalem, in the Old City, on a quiet little side street — a small place, with attendance of about thirty-five guys. I met the head rabbi; his eyes twinkled above his full brown beard. Instinctively, I felt I could trust him. That was how I came to learn at Yeshivas Chochmas HaTorah, under the guidance of the person who would become my rebbe, my mentor, Rabbi Yirmiyahu Shiner.

The night before I moved into the dorm, Shira made a good-bye party in the house for me. It was a beautiful meal. The members of the choir came to say good-bye, all twenty-five of them, and sang a song Shalom had made up for me. The Weiss family kept telling me how much they would miss me. Of course, I would be coming back to visit for Shabbos and vacation, but I felt like I was leaving home for the first time.

The next morning I said an emotional good-bye and thank you to Shira, gave Yanky and Eli hugs, and twirled Huvi and Avigail around the room until they were red from laughter. Then we all packed my belongings in the trunk of Shalom's car. Shalom was going to drive me to my new yeshivah. We drove out of Tzefas exactly seven months to the day that I had arrived, me with my own tefillin, siddur, and Chumash, on the way to the next stage in the exciting life of Keith Caseman.

Several hours later, we pulled into the parking lot of the Old City of Jerusalem. Shalom took out a luggage wheeler he'd brought along, and we wheeled my bags straight to the yeshivah building, up the stairs, and into the room I was shown. Shalom helped me unpack and hang my clothes up. Then we said good-bye once again, with a bear hug that went on for two minutes. Then, finally, Shalom left.

The Old City of Jerusalem is one of the coolest places in the world. Its white stone houses built in all sorts of shapes are separated by winding, shady little streets. A big square in the middle is where most of the action is; friends meet one another and catch up on the news, and guys play football as dogs run on the grass all around. A tunnel cuts through ancient Roman ruins where your voice will echo if you yell and you can picture the lions emerging from the door at the far wall opposite you to fight the gladiator. Eventually, one comes to a row of nice stores selling jewelry, artwork, and T-shirts. There are yeshivos, pizza parlors, and even a deli.

There are world-famous institutions of learning with fantastic views from their roofs. There is the Tower of David with its museum, and across the mountain is the ancient cemetery Har HaZeisim, Mount of Olives. One can walk along the Great Wall of Jerusalem and examine bullet holes left over from the Six Day War. If one travels with a group, he can check out the Arab *shuk* and bargain with the shopkeepers there.

The most interesting events take place there, such as *kiddush levanah* gatherings complete with musical accompaniment held beneath the stars. There are lectures to be heard twenty-four hours a day on every topic under the sun. The Kabbalists call it home, as do Sephardim, Ashkenazim, Chassidim, Mizrachi, and anyone in between. The curving stone structure of the Churvah shul stands out over the Old City like a benevolent angel making sure all is well.

Then, if you walk down the cobblestones past the bank and the jewelry store, past the little cafés and down the steps between Yeshivat HaKotel and Aish HaTorah, you come to an observation deck; and there, spread out in front of you, is the Kosel. The Western Wall. A beacon to Jews the world over, a monument to those lost sons who know they long for something but do not know what. I stood on the lookout point and watched all the people down below hurrying to get close to their Master, and I, too, began to hurry. It was time for *minchah*. After davening I said a special thank you to God for directing me along this path, helping me meet all these special people, and putting me in the right place to learn. I also asked that my parents should come to appreciate what I was doing, since our relationship had never improved, and it hurt me tremendously. Then I kissed the wall and returned to my yeshivah.

Since I'd saved up most of what Shalom had paid me while in Tzefas, I was doing pretty well financially. I also had money I'd won in all my racing competitions. It was springtime and I was so happy to have found such a great yeshivah. The yeshivah was in a very modern building, with state-of-the-art speakers on the walls for lectures and gleaming dark wood furniture. We took pride in our school and took extremely good care of the building and dorms.

The *beis midrash* had that special feeling that comes to a room where people devote their lives to serving God. I was able to sit and learn with concentration for hours at a time there, my wooden book holder in front of me with a Talmud or a Mishnah, swaying over it, saying the words over and over to myself. Learning Chumash, especially with English translation, wasn't so difficult for me. I enjoyed reading through our history — Kayin and Hevel, the flood, our forefathers, the twelve tribes — and I enjoyed Rashi very much. Nach remained a favorite, and, by learning some each day, I was able to get through a few of the *sefarim*.

The *shiurim* in Chochmas HaTorah were excellent. We had Rabbi Zlotkin on Mishnah, whose brilliant explanations that never ceased to impress me. Rabbi Silver taught Jewish history and halachah with a style that would have been an asset to any college professor. I later found out that he actually had been a professor of philosophy at U.C.L.A. and had discovered Judaism on a sociological trip to Israel, where his philosophical arguments had been shredded to pieces by the staff of Aish HaTorah.

Rambam and *hashkafah* were given by "Teddy" Berger, who told us to forget the "rabbi" part on the first day we met him. He enthralled us with his insights into *Derech Hashem*, Maharal, and *Hilchos Teshuvah* of the Rambam. Before Yom Kippur, there was a waiting list to get into his *Reishis Chochmah Shaar HaYirah* class, which supposedly had guys crying like babies.

All these classes were great. However, the most important class, and the one I understood the least, was Gemara by the *rosh yeshivah*, Rabbi Yirmiyahu Shiner.

Although I tried and tried, the concepts eluded me. I'd forget the meaning of the Aramaic words minutes after I learned them, and I couldn't figure out what on earth the Talmud's point was! I stayed up late, got up early, had special tutoring sessions with other guys, but it just wouldn't penetrate. I couldn't see how other people were able to analyze situations with such clear minds, cutting through confusion to reach clarity, while I continued plodding along at the bottom of the mountain.

Since I'd always been the best at whatever I did, it was tremendously humiliating! But I didn't give up, hoping that, sooner or later, something would hit me and it would sink in.

The rabbis and the boys kept encouraging me, but as nice as they all were, I didn't have anyone whom I considered to be a true friend. I missed my parents and all my friends from back home. But, by now, the yeshivah felt very much like home, and at least I could go to Rabbi Shiner any time I had a problem. Months passed and I was dramatically improving in all subjects, but I still couldn't get a grip on Gemara at all.

Shabbos was difficult. Since I had become used to spending

Shabbos with Shalom, Shira, and the kids, I found spending Shabbos with the other guys lacking in family spirit, and I looked forward to the weekends when I was able to travel to Tzefas. Slowly, I met other families from different places and I started going to families in the Old City, Maalot Dafna, and Sanhedria for meals.

My favorite time of the week was Thursday night, *mishmar* night. After supper, we'd all gather in the *beis midrash* where Teddy would give out our work for the night. Every Thursday night it was a different topic. One week it was about reciting the Shema, and Teddy gave out papers on what the Talmud had to say on the subject, what the *Minchas Chinuch* had to say, and what the actual laws were in regard to Shema. We'd pair up and spend a good four hours getting into it, dissecting the different opinions. Afterwards, Teddy gave a lecture tying it all together. When it was all over, at around two in the morning, there would be pizza and ice cream or *schwarma* and fries — a reward and a little incentive.

One Thursday night, six months after my arrival in the yeshivah, Teddy came in and gave out papers. The topic was "When will the Messiah come?" I jumped into the sources, looking up what the commentaries had to say on the subject. All went smoothly up to the Rambam. I couldn't understand what he was saying. Try as I might, I wasn't getting anywhere! The lecture afterwards which usually cleared things up for me just made everything cloudier.

When everyone left to the dining room I stayed in my seat, wondering if I would ever really be able to learn. Not just Chumash with Rashi. I wanted to learn a difficult passage in the Talmud, dissect the Rashi, find where he argued with the *Tosafos*, and then explain the difference in understanding between them. I wanted to really learn! What good was my sitting here all this time if I couldn't get to the depths of the Torah?

Tears came to my eyes. All these rabbis had a flash of fire in their eyes when they taught; that was where I wanted to be. Right then and there I prayed to God to give me the key to the door of knowledge.

When a prayer is said with the utmost concentration and sincerity, it is always heard. I was heard and answered!

There was a tap on my shoulder, and I looked up to see a boy of about twenty-one standing there beside me. "Excuse me," he said. "I couldn't help overhearing your pleading with Hashem to give you clarity." I hadn't realized I was talking aloud. Shocked, I listened in silence as he continued, "Nothing happens in this world for no purpose, and if I, who don't learn here, just happened to come in and overhear something so private, there must have been a very good reason for it.

"Perhaps," he said, as he struggled out of his overcoat and scarf and put his black hat on one of the tables, "I could be of some help to you." He was tall and muscular, well built, with straight black hair and blue eyes, and he was dressed well, his shirt pressed and shoes shined. "By the way," he said, as he extended his hand to me, "I'm Zack."

Chapter Thirteen

Zack. With that one word, my life changed yet again. Zack took me out of my state of returnee to Judaism, a boy with minimal skills, and opened my mind to the beauty of Torah. He was a giant of a guy, a role model, a teacher with unlimited patience. That first night we sat together in the now quiet *beis midrash* and I took out the sheets again, and Zack went through them with me step by step until the Rambam became as clear to me as water. He was sent straight from heaven to show me the way.

He had been on his way back to his yeshivah from the Kosel, but the night was cold and rainy, and he decided to take shelter in my *beis midrash*, which he had passed by many times but never entered. He was funny, he was smart, he was handsome. Most of all, he was my friend.

For the first time in a long while I had a friend, and, wonder of wonders, Zack felt the same way. Two people from totally different parts of the world, with different talents, ideas, backgrounds, degrees of religion — in short, nothing in common — met; and it was as if something clicked between us and we knew this friendship was meant to be. He taught me how to learn, plain and simple. How to open a *gemara* and delve into it like a swimmer throwing himself into the waves. How to look at a Rashi.

"Tell me what Rashi is asking, Keith, because he's always asking something. Go over the Gemara again; if you want to get *Tosafos*, the Gemara has to be on your fingertips. Where does the Ritva differ from the Rashba, Keith? Where do they agree? Use your mind! Find the extra words in the *rishon*. Show me them, and I'll show you why they're not extra. What is the Rambam saying? Is he agreeing with the Rambam in the other chapter?"

We learned philosophy, *mussar,* the works of the Chafetz Chaim. I would go to his yeshivah some nights; sometimes he'd come to me. But we learned every night. Slowly there was a turnaround. I sensed it in myself. When I opened up a *sefer,* I was no longer afraid. My confidence increased by leaps and bounds. My mind was much sharper; the ideas I generated were usually right on target. Zack always had time for me — and, in return, I was there for him. When he wanted to talk to me about something that bothered him, I listened with empathy and tried to be there as much as I could.

Finally, I had someone to hang out with. He took me to his friends and relatives for Shabbos, and after the Friday night meals we would go for long walks in the crisp, chilly nights of Jerusalem, as raindrops dripped off the trees lining the sidewalks and hit me on the eyelashes, making me blink. He was my brother, and he believed in me, and that alone made me succeed.

Chanukah arrived. After candle lighting, Zack came over and we learned the *Beis HaLevi* on Chanukah and the laws of lighting the candles, while the menorahs shone by the window, flickering, throwing their lights into the darkness outside. Afterwards, we took a bus to the homes of the rabbis of my yeshivah, since a different one made a party each night. They were all beautiful evenings. The party at Teddy's house was really special

— the boys sang, Teddy's wife served latkes, and Teddy's speech about Chanukah was so enlightening.

I also accompanied Zack to his *rosh yeshivah*'s party. Rabbi Borenstein, who had already met me, gave me a warm greeting when we arrived. The room's lights were blazing, and a silver menorah stood proudly on the windowsill. Chanukah songs were playing on the stereo. The *rebbetzin* served a full meal and the rabbi spoke about the Greeks of then and their equivalent today. "They haven't vanished; they're alive and well in the five interlocking circles of the Olympics," he thundered.

"When a *bachur* stays up all night to see some goy bash another goy over the head and throw him into the snow so that he can grab the ball and make a touchdown, then the Greeks are the winners. Our job today is to let the little glowing lights of the menorah overcome the huge torch of the Olympic runner, to let the Jewish people stand up to the Greeks in our time."

He mesmerized us. Then they dimmed the lights, until we could just make out each other's faces in the semidarkness, and we sat and sang by the flickering flames of the menorah and a few lamps here and there illuminating the blackness of *galus*. We sat together and sang and sang, bringing one another *chizuk* with our closeness.

All the talks and the encouragement helped me continue to learn seriously after Chanukah. And the memories of that holiday remained with me throughout the cold weeks that followed.

Not only was I changing inside — I was looking a wee bit different on the outside, too. My once-long blond hair was now cut in a shortish style. My jeans were replaced by either dark cotton or dress pants, and instead of T-shirts and sweatshirts I began to wear button-down shirts, usually white. I was now learning with Zack for three hours every day at his yeshivah and I was starting to fit in there quite nicely. My tzitzis hung down over my pants, my shoes were shined.

If I had been shown a picture of myself a year and a half earlier, I would have thought it was insane.

Purim came — the wild, happy, crazy day. A day to let loose, to dress up, to drink, and to have a great time. Zack took the mitzvah of drinking on Purim very seriously. Once he talked about it with me, I took it seriously, too. After the megillah reading, my yeshivah put on a Purim play, which was set in a faraway place where the king decreed that the Jews were only allowed to keep one holiday, either Chanukah or Purim. It was latkes versus hamentaschen; which to pick? The rabbi of the country *paskened* that two teams would play the country's national sport, a game called Kiddush; one team for Chanukah, one for Purim, and the winner would decide!

While all this was going on, the king, who was in the stand to watch the game, started choking on his hamentaschen, which gave the rabbi the chance to say that if the king wanted to live, he must abolish the decree and maybe Purim would forgive him! And since some burning oil had almost spilled on the king on the way to the game, he interpreted the choking as a sign from heaven to abolish his weird plot.

Afterwards someone got up and sang a song in rhyme, making fun of everything going on in the yeshivah. Then we went out to collect *tzedakah* and had a wild time.

The next day I woke bright and early. After davening and hearing the Megillah again, I put on my grasshopper costume and arranged the *mishloach manos* I had bought for my rabbis, friends, and Zack. Then I went in search of a bottle of sweet white wine. If it was a mitzvah to get drunk on Purim, I wanted to fulfill that mitzvah the whole day! I chugged down half of the bottle right away, then found some guys and started dancing.

Within a very short time, I was high. I saw Teddy in the hall-

way, grabbed him in a hug, and escorted him to my room where I ceremoniously handed him his *mishloach manos*. Purim gave me such a great feeling! Why didn't we do it more often? I announced to the world at large my intentions of taking the number two bus to deliver my package to Rabbi Silver. A boy named Jules said he'd come with me to protect me from myself. I found that to be very amusing and showed them all how to walk a straight line, while balancing a pitcher on my head. It was quickly decided that I needed fresh air, and fast.

We walked to the number two bus stop. The bus arrived and we boarded. I pinched the driver's cheek while giving him a sour stick; he smiled back and wished me Happy Purim. I advanced through the crowded bus, singing "*L'chayim*," Jules behind me ready for anything. Before long, the whole bus was full of Purim spirit. Someone even tried dancing, but you can imagine how that worked on the curvy streets of Yerushalayim!

Finally, at around 2:00, I met up with Zack to go to his rebbe for the Purim *seudah*. At this point I was far gone, my head spinning all around, enjoying every second of the day. I ran over to Zack when I saw him and put my arms around him in a giant hug. Then the drunk and the sober made their way to the Purim *seudah*, arm in arm. Zack was in a pretty expansive mood, as best as I can recall, laughing and singing. I'm sure he was on the intoxicated side himself.

Rabbi Borenstein greeted us at the door of his apartment. He shook Zack's hand and, in my inebriated state, I felt the only acceptable thing to do was to kiss his white beard.

All this while I was hanging on to some sort of bubble, which had been in my hand almost the whole day. Now I relinquished my hold on it and allowed myself to be led off to the table for my first real food of the day. What a meal! What costumes, dancing, singing, magic tricks, and Torah speeches. But I was feeling a little queasy — and my head! There were two of everything around me. I tried to put my hand around Zack's shoulder, only to find I was hugging a bowl of ice cubes. It was at that point that I decided, or maybe it was decided for me, that now was a good time to go back to the yeshivah.

The only problem was no taxi wanted to stop for me. I was dressed like a grasshopper and was being supported by two people, and I looked like I was going to lose everything in me at any second!

Finally, a taxi stopped. Zack shoved me into the back of the cab, where I lay across the seat and wished for a shower. The taxi driver didn't want to leave since he was sure I was going to throw up in his car's clean interior. Rabbi Borenstein and Zack insisted I would do no such thing. At some point in the argument, I felt an extreme need to get rid of a huge quantity of unnecessary alcoholic beverages inside me, and I was just barely able to open the back door before it came rushing out. Off into the distance I could still hear them arguing over whether I was going to dirty the taxi or not!

Finally, I finished, whereupon Zack informed the driver that now we could really go. We drove off on our merry way, singing, laughing, and being immature for a little while longer. The next thing I knew it was morning.

When Pesach vacation arrived, I decided that it was high time I got on a boat again. Zack and I traveled to Herzlia, where we rented a sailboat for the day. I took it far out to sea, until the beach was barely visible. We suntanned and relaxed. That water! I can't begin to explain its power over me! We stayed out until it was time for *minchah* and then I brought us swiftly back to shore. It had been a good day.

Chapter Fourteen

West Bank, Israel

The stillness of the night was broken by the raspy sound of a loudspeaker calling the faithful to their prayers. A steady stream of worshipers filled the ancient mosque for the first of the day's five prayers.

A town like any of the myriad other little villages in the Tulkarm area, Jamalkia was home to perhaps two hundred families who had lived there for generations. Its mountainous streets were divided by stone walls used to mark boundaries. Each plot of land was owned by a different family whose dwellings consisted mainly of small, single-story homes. There were a few larger residences which belonged to the wealthier inhabitants of the village, but on the whole the houses were modestly built, with TV antennas on their roofs. The roads were mostly dirt, muddy in the winter, cracked and dry in the summer.

The mosque was the tallest building in the village by far; its crescent symbolized the simple workers' fervent belief in their religion. There was one main street in the middle of the village where the marketplace was.

On Friday, the holy day of the week, the village's entire population was found in the mosque, listening with bated breath to the fiery words of their *imam*, Achmed Al Tirayni. He would preach from the suras of the Koran, speaking about the unity of all the Arab people and decrying the pitiful situation of the poor refugees who lived in squalor and filth in the refugee camps. The crowd would respond in kind, and the plate that was passed around for their brothers in the refugee camps would be filled almost immediately.

On Saturday morning, the men would be found in the village coffee shop, drinking tiny cups of strong Turkish coffee and smoking their narghiles, some squatting on their haunches around the backgammon table. The radio would spit out raucous, noxious propaganda, but the villagers reacted peacefully.

In all the villages around them, recruitment was happening at a feverish pace. Every family had someone in the armed forces, either in Hamas or Islamic Jihad. Every day news of boys who had left their childhood homes in search of paradise, believing that the road to heaven lay in a bloody haze, reached their village. But it didn't matter to the villagers. In the village of Jamalkia no Israeli tank had ever rumbled since the Six Day War for one simple reason.

None of their boys had ever so much as thrown a rock at a bus. No suicide bombers or recruiters came from the area. This village liked its peacefulness and stayed with it; and, in return, it was left alone by the Israelis. Life was good for all concerned.

There is a saying that goes, "Nothing lasts forever." And so it was here also.

On the fourth Friday of the month, the mosque was even more crowded than usual; there was standing room only. That morning, a gleaming black Mercedes had driven into the village with a delegation of prominent men who had come to impart a vital message. The crowd watched in nervous anticipation as the three distinguished gentlemen made their way up to the

speaker's platform. Two of them wore standard Arab dress, loose, flowing robes and kaffiyehs on their heads. The third looked very put together in a dark gray business suit and silk tie, his black hair heavily streaked with gray. The *imam* ascended the podium and the crowd quickly hushed.

"My brothers," he began, his voice shaking with excitement, or was it fear? "I have the exalted honor of presenting to you today a few of the men who make our race so glorious." He proceeded to introduce the two sheikhs who were standing behind him as upholders of the tiger of the nation, Hamas, and the third man as the talented, dedicated, right-hand man of all the important people they had ever heard of. He went on and on with nary a pause for breath until it was understood by all that this man was extremely important and they were to listen properly to everything he had to say.

The man approached the *imam*. They embraced with apparent love, displaying true Moslem brotherhood with a kiss on both cheeks. Then the man began to speak.

The people had never heard anyone like him before — such silken presentation and honeyed words; he made Al Tirayni sound like a child in comparison!

He began by praising the village for its peaceful way of life, which was known far and wide. The villagers basked in the praise. When he called their village a model for the Arab world to emulate, their pride knew no bounds.

"However," he continued, wagging his finger at them, "we are not at peace now. We are now at war; and, at times like these, being peaceful is not a benefit.

"How can it be," and here his voice rose, "that Arab boys everywhere are being slaughtered by the thousands, and from this village not a single boy has seen the dust of battle? The lions of Hamas are fighting until their last breath, while the people here are living in comfort and luxury. The boys of the surrounding villages are going to paradise for fighting the infidels, while the people here...." He didn't want to continue.

The simple villagers were ashamed but still obstinate. He continued with his entreaty for boys to enlist from Jamalkia, promising that, of course, they would reap the benefits of their actions. The two gentlemen behind him were backers of the organization, and they would be happy to send in a recommendation for something to be done for the village in return for a marked change in attitude. "Maybe," and here he paused for effect, "maybe a paved road for the village." But, before all that, he wanted to see a clear difference in their behavior.

He wanted to see their glorious youths, lusty and strong, marching off to battle in army fatigues, their weapons at their sides — only then would he be satisfied.

A subdued mass left the mosque. No one spoke, all afraid to talk while the visitors were still in attendance. As if with one mind, the families headed toward their homes for safety.

The Arab mentality can be quite factionalized. When inspired, they will pledge huge sums of money, give their children to be human mine testers, and blow themselves up for what they believe is the glory of the prophet. On the other hand, once this initial feverish interest has waned, the chance of gathering together some money or getting volunteers for Jihad becomes extremely low. It is virtually impossible to get the average Arab (once the enthusiasm has cooled off) to change his way of life.

Two days later the village was back to normal, having all but forgotten about sending its sons away. When the villagers thought about the situation at all, they hoped, in the back of their minds, that they would not be bothered again. It was not to be. The gleaming black Mercedes would be back.

Chapter Fifteen

Sinai Desert

The last notes of the morning service lingered in the air and finally faded. Nicole, now clad in nun's habit, carried a tray with the Mother Superior's breakfast on it to the Mother Superior's office. She knocked on the heavy door and was bade entrance.

"Good morning, Nicole," the Mother Superior greeted her warmly.

"Good morning, Reverend Mother," Nicole said in return, not as cheerfully.

"What's wrong, my child?" asked the Mother Superior, looking at her with concern. "Are you perhaps not sleeping well?"

"No," said Nicole, "nothing like that is bothering me." She put the breakfast tray down and crossed her arms over her chest.

"So what's the matter?"

"I'll tell the Reverend Mother what the matter is," burst out Nicole. "I came to this place so that I could come to an understanding of my life and my religion, to banish all the questions from my heart. But it's not working, not at all. My doubts just multiply until my mind is so full of them at times that there is no room for anything else."

"But didn't you speak to elderly Father Matties?" protested the Mother Superior. "Wasn't he of any help?"

"No," said Nicole sullenly. "Not only didn't he help me, but he even added to my doubts. He spent an hour trying to prove to me something about the end of days from the New Testament, when I had asked him about something else entirely. And then, when I told him my biggest questions had not been answered, he got all insulted, and out came an hour-long speech about faith. I'm sorry; I refuse to have faith any longer if I can't get the most elementary rudiments of religion clear." She paused. "And I don't think anyone else around here has a clear understanding of our most basic ideas either!"

The Mother Superior narrowed her eyes at Nicole. "What do you mean?" she asked sternly.

"Well," said Nicole, "just yesterday, I asked a visiting priest from Jerusalem a very simple question about an apparent contradiction I noticed in the proofs of when the Messiah came, and he couldn't give me an answer, so he, too, went on a rambling three-hour discourse on the goodness of belief!"

"Yes," smiled the Mother Superior, "Brother Edward does tend to be rather lengthy in his sermons sometimes."

"Yes," retorted Nicole, "especially if he feels that he has just been made to look like a fool. Not only that," she continued, close to tears, "but a week ago I asked one of the older nuns, Sister Sylvia, a simple question about the Sabbath and why we don't keep it the way it was written in the Bible. She slapped me across the face and hissed, 'We've had enough of your heretical questions around here, Sister Nicole! Either desist from your terrible ideas and find some faith, or go find yourself some other people to pervert!'

"I stood there stunned, my cheek stinging from the slap. Even if I do get carried away sometimes, doesn't it say to turn the other cheek? It certainly doesn't say slap your fellow sister who is asking an innocent question because she truly wishes to understand!"

The Mother Superior stood up, went around her desk to where the distraught girl stood crying, and took her in her arms. "One day you will look back at all this and smile because by then you'll have found faith."

"I don't think so," said Nicole, stepping out of the Mother Superior's embrace. "I was hoping to find meaning for my life here, but I don't think I ever will. I've decided to leave."

"Where will you go?" asked the Mother Superior.

"To Jerusalem," said Nicole.

"Oh," said the Mother Superior. "I can give you a recommendation to any of the fine institutions located there."

"I don't think that will be necessary," said Nicole. "I hardly imagine Jewish schools have much use for the recommendation of a Catholic Mother Superior."

"Jewish schools!" croaked out the astonished woman.

"Yes," said Nicole. "Perhaps in the mother of all religions, I'll finally find my place."

She waited for her taxi alone, a pitiful creature, her few bags lying at her feet on the rocky ground outside the convent. The beaming sun shone its powerful rays onto the barren sandy land, which watched impassively as the taxi drove away and Nicole rode back to civilization, hoping desperately to find the meaning behind it all.

How could she even begin to describe the feeling of finally discovering the truth? It was as if she had been imprisoned in a dark dungeon whose thick stone walls hadn't allowed in the smallest sliver of sunlight. She had come up from the depths of the ocean and was now breathing in as much fresh air as she could.

The teachers in Ahavas HaTorah were so unlike any others she encountered in the past. These actually relished questions, rather than being afraid of them. Whenever she asked anything, they would dive into the issue no matter how complex it was and guide her through it until she arrived at a clarity of thought and a joyfulness of spirit. She'd found the school through a stroke of good fortune — it had been recommended by a passing stranger she'd questioned in Jerusalem's Old City. After one day she knew she'd found a very special place; after a few months she realized she'd found her way of life.

Not that they hadn't tried to dissuade her. On the contrary, the teachers in Ahavas HaTorah had informed her that there was no reason for her to convert. They explained to her that God desired nothing more from her than moral behavior. She begged to be allowed to stay. She cried as she told them of her lifelong search for meaning, and they began to accept her sincerity. She loved it at this school! There was such happiness to be found over here; it was so different from the rest of the world's perception of religion as a burden. For these people, not only wasn't it a burden, it was something beloved, something cherished!

Now she lived in a dorm full of girls as eager to learn as she, girls as full of questions as she was. It was such a pleasure to finally begin to understand God's words and His world. Here in this school, after she had proved she wasn't coming with bad intentions, she had been accepted and taught and loved. All her questions had answers, and her search for meaning was coming to an end. The long-buried pain inside Nicole Salvador at last began to diminish as she learned more and more about becoming a religious Jew.

The months passed quickly. I was learning very well, growing in all aspects; my friendship with Zack continually deepening. Zack was now twenty-three, and I was almost twenty-one. I was an inch or two taller, a little broader in the shoulders, and I took life pretty seriously. My relationship with my parents, unfortunately, never straightened out. Although my father called every so often to find out how I was doing, my mother never stopped being antagonistic toward my way of life.

Two weeks before my twenty-first birthday, Rabbi Shiner called me into his office. I wondered what he could possibly want. Everything was fine; *chavrusas* were going well, especially since I was learning with Zack most of the day. I entered his office and greeted him happily.

"Ah, Keith, how are you?"

"I'm fine, Rabbi, what's up?"

"I'll tell you. I just got a call from a friend of mine, Rabbi Lazarus, over at Ohel Rivka."

He had my attention now. "Yes?"

"He told me about a certain girl by the name of Karen, and, after hearing how he described her, I felt she might very well be the right girl for you."

The right girl for me? A *shidduch*? Marriage? That wasn't what I'd been expecting to hear. I was quiet for a few minutes, turning the idea over in my mind. I was going to turn twenty-one soon. I loved the yeshivah, but there were times when I longed for a place of my own, a home, a family. My parents were far, far away, separated by thousands of miles and an even bigger gap in values and lifestyles. A family of my own, a Torah life, a wife, kids...it sounded like a pretty good idea!

I turned my attention back to Rabbi Shiner, who'd been watching me closely. "So tell my about her," I grinned.

"Before she became religious, she excelled at water sports, just like you. In fact, she was a semifinalist on the U.S. Olympics women's swimming team."

I was impressed.

"Personality sounds just about right," continued Rabbi Shiner. "Not too loud, but exciting and fun, and also serious about her Judaism." He looked at me over his glasses. "Well, how does it sound?"

"It sounds great, Rabbi! Does she know about me?"

"She will very soon; first I wanted to see if you'd be interested; then I thought I'd let Rabbi Lazarus take care of his part of the game."

He swiveled around in his black leather chair and looked out the window at the view of the Moslem Quarter. "You know, Keith, I'm very happy with the progress you've made since you've come here. If this works, it will be a very satisfactory ending to a beautiful story. I will let you know what's what as soon as I know."

I left his office walking on air. My fingers were already playing wedding music. This must be right; it sounded so promising!

I knew Zack had been out on a number of dates, so I consulted with him for all the do's and don'ts. He told me a few of his *shidduch* stories, and I told him about the dates I had been on back in Illinois. After picking up the girl, I'd take her to my boat and sail out into the lake. I'd time it for twilight, when the sun would be setting, turning into a crimson ball, descending into the silvery water. I'd put on some music, a mix of different sound tracks I'd collected which fit the mood, and take a bottle of champagne out of the little fridge on my boat.

Zack laughed. "That sounds very sweet, a good idea for the night you propose maybe. Most definitely not the first date."

That night Rabbi Shiner called me back into his office. "It's arranged, Keith."

"Great, Rabbi."

"Since it's your first date, I took the liberty of setting up the venue. How does the King David Hotel at 7:30 on Monday evening sound?"

"Fine with me," I said. It was as good a place to meet as any. "How will I recognize her, Rabbi?"

"Oh, right," he said. "She has dark blond hair, she's about five foot two, she'll be wearing something blue, and she'll be standing by the elevators holding a folded newspaper and an umbrella. Just kidding about the last part." His face turned serious and he looked me in the eyes. "Good luck, Keith." I thanked him and left the office.

Monday dawned drizzly and gray. It didn't bother me; my philosophy is the cloudier it is in the daytime, the darker it is at night, and the brighter the lights shine. I just knew this was going to be fantastic. I made up my mind to dress casually. No suit or tie; nice pair of pants, grayish black, white shirt, cable knit sweater, and my raincoat on top. I hoped the girl wouldn't mind. Just to make sure, I asked Rabbi Shiner to call up and ask. "No problem," he told me.

I took a shower, brushed my hair, and got ready for the date, making sure I had enough money for whatever I might need. At 6:45 I was ready to leave.

I decided to walk to the King David Hotel. It was one of those perfect Jerusalem nights. Pitch black sky; the stars, white pinpoints studding the heaven. The sidewalks were wet and shiny from the rain that had fallen that afternoon. A brisk wind blew as I left Jaffa Gate and walked past the Dan Pearl Hotel.

There was a spring in my step, that exciting feeling that

anything could happen. Would it be a great date or would it not be a great date; that was the question! I passed the Hilton Hotel and continued past the car rental places and the art galleries. I reached the King David at 7:20 — just enough time to scout around a little.

The first place I saw was a bar with wooden furniture and a masculine feel; a place a man might go to have a cigar. The lounge was very open; no privacy. Then I noticed a restaurant off to the side. I walked in. On the other side of the room, glass doors led off into a magnificent garden, lit up with soft lights, which called to me to explore.

Unfortunately I didn't have the opportunity, since it was about time for me to get back to the front of the hotel and meet her. I walked through the revolving doors and positioned myself right outside them to the left, my hands in my pockets.

All at once, she was there, walking toward me, the lights throwing her shadow across the cobblestones that led up to the hotel. I could hear the music playing in my mind as she approached, violins soaring up to the heavens. I could see a blue outfit beneath her coat.

She reached me, and I said, "Hi, I'm Keith."

"I'm Karen," she returned.

We entered the hotel and I said, "Let's go for a walk in the garden, all right?"

"Great idea," she said.

We went out through the glass doors, down the stairs, and into a place of sculptured bushes and flowerbeds, a trimmed green lawn, and, off to the side, the pool, which was empty. We sauntered along, getting to know each other.

"Where are you from, Karen?" I asked her.

"I'm from Manhattan," she answered. "Ever been there?"

"My parents took me a few times, especially to and from races."

"Where did you used to race?"

I told her about the races I'd been in and how they were instrumental in my becoming religious. I didn't go into great detail, though, just gave her an abridged version of my last big races.

"I also used to travel a lot for my swimming meets," she said. "When I wasn't on the road I was practicing! We used to practice so much that I hardly had any free time."

The conversation changed to family issues. "How did your parents take it when you decided to become religious?" I asked her.

She smiled. "My dad is one of those rare people who truly believe that everyone is entitled to live their life the way they see fit, so he is fine with it. My mom wasn't so fine with it. She took me with her on endless morning excursions, as she called them, to Fifth Avenue, in an attempt to show me all the things I'd be giving up by leaving that world.

"She didn't realize that the more I saw the nicest things money could buy, the less I was interested in them. So now when we talk it's like, 'Karen, honey, how are you, sweet? Gotta run and meet Terry for lunch. Our foundation is having a meeting soon and we simply must plan the color scheme.' "

I burst out laughing. She smiled at me and then turned serious and said, "It's a shame that our interactions are so superficial because we used to have such a beautiful relationship."

"Well," I said, "my mother is so upset that I'm here that she has barely talked to me for over two years! And I don't know why she's so angry at Judaism. It's very strange."

Conversation came easily to us. We spoke about her two brothers, one a lawyer, the other a musician in the New York Philharmonic Orchestra. We discussed hobbies, music we liked, books we enjoyed, her ambitions — she had gone to college and wanted to work in her field of speech therapy — and our friends.

I told her about my best friend, Zack, and that night long ago when I cried up to heaven to help me; how Zack had appeared like an angel and came to my rescue. We spoke for two hours, neither one of us wanting to end the evening. After leaving the King David at about 10:00, we walked the streets, talking and talking. Finally, at about 12:30, I took her back to her school in a taxi and said good night.

I don't know how I returned to the yeshivah. It was an open miracle because I certainly wasn't aware of where I was going. When the taxi left me off outside the Old City, I walked without seeing back to my dorm room.

What a date! What a connection! I felt like screaming with joy, but that's not such a great idea at 1:30 in the morning. The relationship would go places. I had no question about that. It was just a matter of time. I wished my parents were here and part of this. Unbidden, my thoughts turned to my last visit home.

My father had met me at the airport, looking in surprise at my conservative style of dress — my short haircut, my tzitzis, and my black velvet yarmulke. He didn't make any remarks about it, though; that's not his style. He just gave me a hug and a handshake and helped me with my bags to the car.

As we drove down the familiar roads, lined by my friendly oaks still standing strong and waving hello, I felt a certain welcoming feeling. We pulled into the driveway, and there stood my mother — my mother, who had barely spoken to me for the past two years. She smiled at me through the window, but when I got out of the car, her smile froze.

"Did you have to bring that archaic dress home with you, Keith?" she asked angrily.

"Welcome home to you, too," I replied, determined not to respond to her anger. If this was the way she was choosing to handle the situation, then there was nothing I could do about it. I would just be myself and show them that I was still the same Keith.

But it was just terrible, from the first night at supper, when her anger bubbled forth at me for not eating the food she had cooked, and throughout my entire visit. Nothing I could do or say made any difference, and my father didn't bother to back me up even a little. I felt extremely alone and vulnerable.

One morning at breakfast, I lost my cool. We were sitting down to eat — omelets and waffles for them, and a plastic bowl of Cheerios for me — when my mother made another comment. I glanced at her, my eyes filled with tears, and asked her, "What happened to you? You used to be a mother; now you seem to feel your purpose in life is to cause your one and only son as much pain as possible."

I laid my spoon down, stood up, and left the table. After pacing the floor in my room for a few minutes, I started packing my bags. Then I went back down to ask my father to please take me back to the airport, where I would change my ticket, even if it meant losing money, and fly back to Israel.

Before Dad could respond, Mom came over to me. "I'm sorry, Keith. I don't know what came over me. Could you please stay a little longer?"

We went into the den, our old favorite spot for a good talk, by the window overlooking the lake. The curtains moved gently in the wind, and I could see my boat bobbing up and down in the water. My mother sat down in her rocker; I sat down opposite her on the old leather couch.

"Mom, you used to be such an accepting person. How could you, of all people, treat me so badly?"

She started crying. Lowering her head, she said, "I know I've been terrible to you, and I know you're really the same beautiful boy you always were, but I just can't reconcile myself to the fact that these fanatics caught up with you."

"But, Mom, do I seem like such a fanatic?" I asked.

"Keith, you're still young, and I hope you never find out what I mean when I say fanatic; but, believe me, I'm not talking out of hate. I love you, Keith," here she broke down totally, "but I'm afraid that one day you will hate me, so, in order to protect myself, I must erect barriers between us."

I crouched down next to her chair and took her hand, wet from the tears which had dropped on it. "I will never hate you, Mom, please believe me!"

But she had some fear, an illogical fear, that prevented her from being my mother who loved me so much. As much as she wanted me to stay, my very presence was causing her pain, and that made her say hurtful things to me. Although I didn't leave that day in the end, I could hardly wait for my scheduled departure day.

The one nice part of my visit was the time when I took my father out in my sailboat, and we had a man-to-man talk. He admitted that he himself didn't know what had come over my mother, and it was causing him tremendous pain, but I should know that he was behind me all the way.

I didn't speak to Estelle when I was there. I think she was in college, otherwise she probably would have come over. It didn't matter, though. Nothing mattered, if my own mother couldn't find it in herself to give me her genuine smile and say, "Welcome back, Keith; I missed you, honey."

It was a gray day when we drove back to the airport. My oaks didn't wave at me and I ignored them; in some way they had let me down and they knew it. *Good-bye, home of my youth. Let me pull your knife out of my back and go on living.*

I blinked, and my eyes came back into focus. That was then.

I looked out my window at the Silwan Valley, the jumbled houses throwing out a light here and a light there in that jumbled Arab building style, and thought, *This is now. Everything will be just great from here on!*

The next morning I spoke to Rabbi Shiner at breakfast. We sat across from each other with tall, steaming cups of coffee, and he asked, "How did it go?"

I monopolized the rest of the conversation, telling him what we did and how well the conversation had gone.

He smiled, amused at my enthusiasm. "So you want to go out with her again?"

"You could say that again, Rabbi!"

"When shall I set it up for you, Keith?"

"How about two nights from now? The quicker the better!" He promised to do his best, and I thanked him and left.

I went to meet Zack at his yeshivah, where I rehashed the whole thing over again with him. I was so happy.

Rabbi Shiner called me in again later that day and told me it was all arranged for Wednesday night. I should pick Karen up at the bus stop near her school and have a good time.

On Wednesday evening I left the *beis midrash* at 5:30, took a shower, and got ready. Then I called a taxi and we drove to Bayit Vegan. After picking Karen up, I directed the taxi driver to town and we got out near Jaffa Street. We walked into the maze of streets that branch off in all directions.

It was such a beautiful winter night and such great company that I suddenly whistled. Karen turned and looked at me, laughter in her eyes, and said, "I feel exactly the same way."

I took her to Angelo's, my favorite little Italian place in Jerusalem. With its checkered tablecloths, bright pictures, and Italian music, the ambience is conducive to whatever you trying to achieve. The woman who works there smiled and winked at me as she seated us upstairs at a table overlooking the lower level.

The bread, with its garlicky oily taste, always gets me going, and their soup, forget it! Karen, it seemed, liked this kind of food as much as me, and she seemed very much at ease. We talked and talked. I told her about my visit back home and how much I was hurt by my mother. Her reaction was exactly what I needed; she was there for me.

Afterwards she told me some things her family had said when she first changed her lifestyle and what it had done to her. Then we said together, "Enough of this." Her sense of humor came to light as she told me funny stories of her life at school and at her swimming events.

We got our spaghetti melted with cheese and dried tomatoes, the basil shimmering in a sea of olive oil. As Karen expertly twirled some onto her fork, she told me about an amusing incident that happened to her in a little restaurant in Venice.

I told her about England and the storm, painting the picture vividly. I told her about the whirlpools and Captain Bob, and she was enthralled. We sat in Angelo's, the candle flame flickering on the table, talking in low voices while the wind whistled outside the store and Pavarotti serenaded us in a sultry voice.

I explained to her how I realized that Someone up there was guiding us, on that wild lake in England with sheets of water pouring down all around me, and that was my start to the truth.

We sat there companionably, talking quietly together until the red wax candle melted down to the dish and the rest of the patrons went home.

The next few weeks were a crazy couple of weeks. I felt like I was on a roller coaster, moving so fast from thrill to thrill. We must have gone to every good restaurant, nice park, and scenic walk in the city.

We took the bus up to Haifa, strolled along the Hass Promenade, took the cable cars down the mountain, and got to the bottom as the sun set on the water. The next week we went to the naval museum and the science museum and then we went to Park Leumi, where we rented a boat for a few hours. Afterwards we went to Elgoucho's in Ramat Gan for dinner.

I spoke about Karen a lot with Zack and Rabbi Shiner, and both of them were thrilled for me. Our dating couldn't go on much longer; it was time to take it to the next stage. I asked Rabbi Shiner to please find out if she was ready for the big jump. When he called me back into his office, his face was serious.

He leaned back into his chair and, stroking his beard, said, "Keith, as to Karen being ready, she is. However, talking to Rabbi Lazarus, he mentioned something that needs to be looked into. I understand you told Karen that your mother was married to someone else before she married your father. Do you know if she got a *get* from her first husband?"

The question hit me like a ton of bricks! I felt a sharp painful feeling surge through me, and suddenly I knew what it was my mother was so afraid of!

Chapter Sixteen

My fingers trembled as I pushed the buttons on the phone. Twice I had to start dialing over again. Then it was ringing, every ring bringing me closer to what could possibly be a life of pain and anguish. Someone was picking up the phone. "Hello." It was my father's voice.

"Hi, Dad," I said. "Can I please speak to Mom?"

"Hello, Keith. I'll go get her from the garden."

I could hear the footsteps approaching, and then my mother's voice over the lines. "Hello, Keith."

"Mom, I have a question for you."

I heard the sharp intake of breath on the other end of the line. "Yes?" she said.

"Before you were married to Dad, you were married to Kenny Gordon, right?"

"That's correct, Keith."

"Well, when you divorced him, did you obtain a *get*?"

The words hung in the air between us, each word a bullet. My mother's voice, so sure of itself a moment ago, was small and defenseless. "No, I didn't," she said.

Suddenly she was screaming at me, and it was like we were

in the same room. "I told you not to go, I warned you, 'Don't stay there; you'll ruin your life! Those people are fanatics!' But you had tc stay. You knew better. Now what will happen to you? You probably wanted to marry someone, that's why you're asking, right?"

"Yes," I whispered.

"Well, now you won't be able to! Why didn't you listen to me then?"

Something inside me snapped. The tears streamed down my face as I yelled, "How could you do this to me? You just ruined my life! Not just my life; all my future descendants will have the same blemish I have! I can't marry Karen now; you cut off my arm! Why didn't you think a little bit into the future when you made the selfish decision to destroy any children you'd have?"

I ground my fist into my eyes, the sorrow inside me threatening to engulf my entire being. "You know what I am now," I said scathingly. "I can't even say the word; it hurts me too much. I can't marry anyone now. Mom, you killed me, and you would have been happier if I had never become religious, so I wouldn't have known what I am.

"No! To be religious is the correct thing! To be religious is good and right and I'm happy I discovered it. But how could you do something like this when you knew what might happen?! You knew, didn't you?"

"Yes, Keith, I did know, but I didn't take it seriously," she sobbed.

Suddenly, I couldn't bear the knowledge of what I had just found out. I felt heat on my forehead, and a pounding inside me getting stronger and stronger. The phone slipped out of my hand, and I was on the floor.

There were faces around my bed. Zack and Rabbi Shiner

were there. Zack saw me open my eyes and he reached down, pulled me up, and hugged me. I leaned my head on his shoulder and cried like a baby.

"Zack," I choked, "I'm a...I'm a...oh, I can't say it. What's the difference, you know what I am; but Karen doesn't know, and there is no possible way I can tell her. I would just look at her and cry.

"How could I possibly explain to her that my mother went ahead and got married without a *get*, an action that will keep me unmarried forever?" Sobs wracked my body with tidal wave force. I felt as if I would never stop crying.

Rabbi Shiner looked at me with tremendous sympathy. "I'll talk to Karen and break the news to her. But don't think that there's nothing to be done. You're not the first person this has happened to. I've made an appointment for you with one of the greatest experts in the field of Jewish genealogy, Rabbi Baruch Zicherman."

I told Rabbi Shiner whatever I knew about my mother's first marriage and he promised to make some phone calls for me as soon as possible. The next day we drove down to Rabbi Zicherman's yeshivah. I wondered what Rabbi Shiner had found out, but when he didn't volunteer any information I decided to wait and hear what Rabbi Zicherman had to say.

We were shown to Rabbi Zicherman's office by a younger rabbi with a long black beard. Rabbi Zicherman was giving a *shiur* and would be arriving any minute. We waited for him to return in silence.

A few minutes later, Rabbi Zicherman came in. I looked up in surprise. He was the rabbi from the disco boat, so long ago. He looked at me with instant recognition, and his beautiful eyes became so sad. The lines on his brow were so thick they ran into each other; it seemed like he had the world's troubles resting on his shoulders.

"*Shalom aleichem*," he greeted me, taking my clammy hand in his own comforting one. "I understand there is a question regarding your parentage?" His eyes looked at me questioningly.

Rabbi Shiner spoke up. "I wish it was more of a question, Rebbe, but I've spoken to the *beis din* in Boston which was involved with the divorce. When Kenny Gordon, who was the first husband, wouldn't give a *get* unless Joannie, Keith's mother, paid a large sum of money, she refused the *get*.

"Rabbi Bender, the *av beis din*, told me he personally spoke to her for many long hours, trying to convince her, but to no avail. She didn't care about religion that much, and the more he spoke to her, the more antagonistic she became.

"Finally, Rabbi Bender told me, he threatened her that if she didn't get a *get*, the *beis din* would write up a document saying any children she might have would be *passul*."

Rabbi Zicherman sighed. "*Oy, vey*, what will be with *klal Yisrael*; it's a spiritual holocaust!" He turned to Rabbi Shiner. "What about the woman's second marriage, was it kosher? Good witnesses and everything?"

"Unfortunately, yes," said Rabbi Shiner. "It appears that the rabbi who married Keith's parents was an old man who never dreamt that he was being used in such a terrible way. The situation looks quite bleak, Rebbe. What is there to do?"

"What about the first husband; are you sure he is Jewish?"

"I looked into that direction also, Rebbe. I even got in touch with Kenny Gordon's mother, who very indignantly informed me that, of course, her Kenny is a Jew, and how dare I have the temerity to even suggest otherwise. I checked in all directions and I'm at an extreme loss as to what to do next."

I sat there in that sunny office and saw my future crumble in front of my eyes.

Rabbi Zicherman swayed back and forth. Finally he turned

to me. "There are a few more ideas we have to discuss, although now is not the proper time. I want you to go back to yeshivah and learn like you never learned before, and may the *Ribbono shel Olam* be with all of us." He drew me close and added, "Keith, a person never really knows who he should marry. Perhaps Hashem has someone else in mind for you."

I didn't know how to respond to that, so I didn't respond at all. Rabbi Shiner and Zack promised to be in touch, and we left. Me? As soon as I got back to yeshivah, I went to my room, changed into my sweats, got into bed, and stayed there.

It was a week after my meeting with Rabbi Zicherman, and I had woken up late yet again. I just couldn't summon up the energy to pull myself out of bed. Why should I? For what purpose? I knew I should be going to learn with Zack, but I had absolutely zero interest. It was as if my life had ended with that telephone call to my mother. It didn't look like I would be able to get married, and if I couldn't get married and have a home, there would be no warmth in my life. I knew a person's job is to serve Hashem in every situation that he finds himself in, but I hated life now. I felt that I would never be happy again.

There was a knock on the door and Zack walked in. "Hi, Keith, what's up?"

I rolled over, looked up at him, and said, "You know what's up. I'm the most depressed person in the universe, with no chance of changing my situation for the better."

Zack looked down at me. "You need the enjoyment of a good piece of Gemara. When was the last time you really learned?"

"I don't remember," I said.

"C'mon," said Zack, grabbing my hand and pulling me up. "Let's go learn. I think you'll be surprised to find your perspective change a little after you've learned a good couple of hours."

I got dressed reluctantly and followed Zack down to the *beis midrash*, and that old familiar feeling washed over me. There are certain *batei midrashim* whose walls have a tremendous amount of learning in them. The never-ending straining of minds to get to the depths of understanding mix with endless quantities of sweat and tears until the walls release all the emotions so they can be felt by the people who come and learn.

The more learning that takes place in a room, the easier it becomes to continue learning in that same room. The first time I walked into the Mir *beis midrash* I experienced this feeling. My yeshivah's walls obviously hadn't taken in nearly as much, but they still gave off this overpowering learning spell. And so, when I sat down with Zack and we opened up a Gemara, my mind, which hadn't learned properly for a while, rejoiced, and the juices started flowing again.

Soon we had the *sefarim* piled up next to us. The Rambam, the Ritva; it was *leibedik*. Zack uncovered a *machlokes* between Rashi and *Tosafos*, and he remember a *Ketzos* which he thought might very well explain the argument. I had a different interpretation of what the *Ketzos* was saying, so things really heated up. For a while I was able to escape from my misery.

When we finished learning, Zack asked me if I want to take a walk. We walked through the alleyways of the Old City, ascended the stone steps leading to the Churvah Arch, and found an empty bench to sit on.

Zack looked at me with compassion. "I know how hard this is for you, Keith. One day you're getting engaged, and the next you find out you're a.... I'd rather not mention the word."

"You know, Zack," I said, "I keep on hoping that I'll wake up and this whole sorry saga will just be a nightmare. I pinch myself until I'm black and blue, hoping that I'm only sleeping, but no such luck. Sometimes I feel a crazy feeling run through me, as if I'm on walking on the edge of a blade; where one false step could mean the end of my life. I'm hoping for a miracle, but if one doesn't happen, then that knife's edge will get closer and closer, pulling me down, to a place of no return!

"Am I ever going to have a Shabbos table of my own, with my family sitting around it waiting for me to say *HaMotzi*? Will I have the opportunity to host young, mixed-up boys and girls from irreligious homes in my house? Will I ever have any children? Zack, you know how much I love little kids; my heart melts when I see a baby, and now I can never have any of my own.

"Why would Hashem do this to me? I gave up my whole life for Him! I know I gained a new, much better life, but I left my family, my friends, my sailing career, and now I have nothing, not them and not this.

"Remember that rainy night a few years ago, when Hashem directed you into my life after I had sent up a sincere request to Him?"

"Of course," nodded Zack.

"Well, every time I daven and every time I learn, I have another request. I ask Hashem, 'Please let me get married and raise a family in *Klal Yisrael*.' I'm hoping that, just like last time, when Hashem heard me and sent you to mold and develop me into who I am today, He'll hear me now and send the answer. I don't know what He wants from me now, but the only thing I can do is wait."

Zack stroked the short beard he'd been cultivating for the past couple of months, grabbed my hand, and gave it a kiss. "Keith," he said, "I'm privileged to have such an amazing person as a friend. All you really want to do is the will of God. I'm certain that Hashem hears your *tefillos*, and you will be answered at the proper time.

"As for now, until that angel comes and gives you the outline of God's ten-year plan for you, you must learn; you must kill yourself over Torah. You know the only real happiness is in learning and all else is meaningless, but you must internalize this message.

"Come," he said, pulling me to my feet. Feeling exhilarated, we climbed the wall beside us to the roof of the building adjacent to us. We leaped from rooftop to dome to porch, free as the birds, until we landed on one roof where we couldn't go any further. From there we could see into the window of a home.

There was a family sitting around the dining room table eating dinner, the mother ladling out some soup from the pot for her children, the father sitting at the head of the table having a discussion with his oldest son. It was family life at its best. I envied them their connection; but, after talking things out with Zack, I was a lot more hopeful that Hashem would show me my path, which colored stone road I was to travel to reach my particular destination....

For Zack, returning to his yeshivah, life was far from comfortable; in fact, life was wet and cold and windy. When he had left the Old City not too long before, the sky had still been clear and he had opted for the longer route back to his yeshivah. Suddenly, however, the grayest, most swollen of clouds had decided to water the parched earth and proceeded to drench the unsuspecting Zack.

Having no choice, Zack took refuge in an almost empty felafel shop on Shmuel HaNavi Street, where he waited for the storm to abate. Feeling a little more cheerful once he was in the warm, aromatic store, Zack bought a coffee and sat down at one of the tables. Immediately, his mind turned to Keith — Keith of the many talents, Keith of the joyful personality, one of the nicest, most genuine people Zack knew.

As much as he had given Keith, he had gotten back, in learning and in friendship. For Zack, the boy with tons of admirers, finally having a friend added a whole new dimension to his life. When he had been going through a bad time a year before and wasn't getting along with his family, Keith had been there for him. He was a constant reminder that as hard as life got there was always something to look forward to.

Zack remembered the time he had brought up the subject of a Jewish name for Keith. Keith's reaction had been most unexpected. He had explained to Zack that he wouldn't feel honest with himself if he changed his name just so people would think better of him. "I hope I'm a good Jew even with an English name," he said.

Zack respected that honesty. In fact, he admired Keith for his many quality character traits. But he just couldn't figure out why Keith had had to go through such hard times, such difficult challenges. He felt for him. At night, he would lie in bed in the dorm, his mind churning with possible solutions. Keith's pain was like a dagger in his heart, and he thought to himself, *If this is the way I feel, kal vachomer how he must feel.*

Inside the steamy store, with the radio playing cheerful music and the sizzling sound of frying food in the background, it was easy to forget the winter weather outside, and his mind drifted off to....

Camp. That one word will bring a smile to the bearded face of a thirty-five-year-old. Instant visions will appear of campfires at two o'clock in the morning, baseball games in fields slippery after a morning's rain. On Shabbos morning there is *kokosh* cake with a glass of milk before davening if you're not bar mitzvah and after davening if you are.

Camp. Concerts and hiking (and getting lost with your

counselor in the forest); leagues and plays, with the same themes over and over again; night canteen, if you're friendly with an older staff member. Music, *melaveh malkahs*, and trips are all part of the experience. Stories told at night as you're drifting off to sleep, with your laundry bag creating strange shadows on the wooden walls, your counselor pacing back and forth, shining his flashlight on the floor, spinning a tale about Simon Shapiro and a bear or bringing to life a story about a tzaddik from long ago.

There's color war, which nobody wants and yet everyone looks forward to, and Olympics which nobody wants and nobody looks forward to. Prizes for learning and swimming pools full of chlorine. Rowing boats on the lake, having water fights, playing Risk on Shabbos afternoons, and sitting, sweaty and hot, in the dining room on Shabbos morning, waiting for the *seudah* to finish.

Friendships, and pillow fights, and Shoprite in the Catskills, or Mr. Z.'s in the Poconos. Salamanders being sold for fifty cents a piece, comedy and halachah skits, and Friday afternoon staff baseball games. Skunks in the bunks and raccoons in the garbage cans. Golf courses and go-carts. Computers and rock climbing and sometimes batting cages and bumping boats.

No matter how advanced your camp is and how many new enjoyable activities it has to entice you with, camp still boils down to the old awesome event which has been the highlight of every camp summer for the past fifty years — the grand sing. Anyone who has ever stood there with his team wearing a silly cardboard hat and sung his heart out can tell you how it affected him. From the oldest staff member to the youngest boy in Bunk *Alef*, from the coolest kid who never has time for singing to the soloists of both teams, everyone knows that there is nothing more moving than the grand sing.

All this passed through Zack's mind as his thoughts turned

to last summer. As one of the most popular counselors in camp, he was a definite candidate for general in color war, so he wasn't surprised when he was called into the head counselor's office the night before color war was to break out. Sitting in the ratty old camp office, with busted basketballs and games lying around, the cool evening mountain air blowing in through the windows, were the head counselor and the learning director, the dynamic duo who ran the camp.

"Hiya, Zack," they said. "How ya doin'?"

"Great," he answered. They offered him the job and he accepted happily. In the midst of their discussion about who the lieutenant generals were going to be, the head counselor suddenly said, "You know, when I was a teenager I could never have taken such an active role in color war."

Zack looked at him in surprise.

"When I was in high school, I was very unpopular, and with good reason. I didn't have a good attitude towards friendship, and I was always getting into arguments with others. But I wanted to change, and after many years of struggling I've become a different person. Zack, if a person doesn't have it so easy early on — be it with relationships, Torah learning, or anything else — but continues to work on himself and doesn't give up, no matter how many setbacks he has, he will end up vanquishing the negative traits and building himself until he become someone others will want to emulate. If a person approaches a challenge in the right way, he emerges a much stronger person."

Then he went back to discussing the color war teams. But those words about character building had penetrated deep into Zack's mind and stayed there.

They came back to him now as he sat in the greasy felafel shop. Perhaps all this was happening to Keith because at the end of the day, if he stuck through it all, he would emerge a much stronger, more effective, and more developed *ben Torah*. Maybe

Hashem had great plans for Keith, and now He was building him up for the future.

With that comforting thought in mind, Zack said a *berachah acharonah*, put his coat back on, and prepared to brave the wind once more. As he walked outside, he understood why he had heard these insightful words months ago. They were a sign. A sign for his Keith.

Chapter Seventeen

Lebanon

His name was Yassir and he was Jamalkia's wayward son. While all the other boys his age were content to stay in the village, learning the trades of their fathers, Yassir had made it his business to attend high school, not a small achievement for a boy who came from a family of shepherds. He had graduated with top marks and won a scholarship to the university in Beirut. While there, he had been recruited by the PLO faction which existed in the college. A smart, ambitious, and charismatic young man with the bearing of a military leader, he inspired confidence in all those around him.

If you drive four hours from Beirut to the northeast, you will approach a mountainous region. Gradually the roads will get rockier and more difficult to travel on. The farther you go, the trickier the driving becomes, until the road changes into a path and eventually a very narrow trail. The turnoff, when it comes, is extremely easy to miss, unless you happen to be very familiar with the area. And even if you know your way around, you'd better hope your presence in the region is approved, since you're bound to meet up with one of the many patrols which roam the area. Unauthorized visitors usually have a very short stay.

After another quarter of a mile or so, the trail will begin to turn steeply upwards, making a four-wheel drive the vehicle of choice. The wooded area will eventually open up to a cleared patch of land, and off in the distance, if you strain your eyes hard enough, a tall barbed-wire fence can be seen. Guards bearing all sorts of weapons will come over to say hello and give you the once-over. In short, you have reached Camp Jihad.

Yassir underwent intensive guerrilla training at Camp Jihad, where he acquired skills far beyond that of the average PLO member.

He learned "bomb making for dummies," a course given by an elderly Palestinian named Hassan, who was able to put together a bomb with a battery, a few wires, and a toothpick, if necessary. He was taught how to recruit and how to fight hand-to-hand combat. He learned underwater demolition from a Russian naval officer named Alexi. He learned how to assemble rockets and how to use almost every type of weapon, from an M16 to an Uzi submachine gun.

He was instilled with the brutal knowledge that the Arab world was at war and drastic steps were necessary to fight the battle. He was taught how to blend into any crowd, with makeup and contact lenses of every color. Yes, the son had left a country boy, ignorant of the better things in life, and he was returning a suave man of the world.

His most destructive weapon, however, was not all of this; it was his tongue. He was one of the most effective recruiters to be turned out in a very long while.

The question arose — where to send such an accomplished fighter. The higher-ups debated amongst themselves for a while before deciding upon a place that had never done anything for the cause: Jamalkia, Yassir's hometown.

The Bulldozer's men arrived in Israel and checked in at the Dan Pearl Hotel, Jerusalem. Over the next few days they looked into real estate possibilities in the area closest to Nicole's place of residence. By the end of the week, Kevin and his partner, Derek, the boy he'd chosen to accompany him, were comfortably installed in their new apartment, which happened to be conveniently located across the street from Nicole's school, affording them a bird's-eye view of the seminary's front door.

One of them was always at home, keeping on eye on the front door across the street, while the other hung around the neighborhood. They kept in touch with their cell phones, and any time Nicole left her school, one of them was always close behind, tracking where she went and, more importantly, whether she was seeing anybody that the Bulldozer would want to know about.

Nicole, now officially called Nechama, waited at the *rebbetzin*'s door and took a deep breath, summoning up the courage to knock. When she knocked, she heard the *rebbetzin* bidding her to enter. Nicole walked into the office, a room she was very familiar with.

Rebbetzin Greenberg was on the phone. She motioned for Nicole to have a seat while she completed the conversation. Nicole looked around at the homemade curtains hanging over the windows and the beautiful paintings and pictures of *rabbanim* that graced the walls. She gazed at the family photos displayed on the desk and sighed.

Finally Rebbetzin Greenberg completed her telephone call and turned to Nicole. "How are you, dear?" she asked.

Nicole smiled at the older woman. "I'm fine, *Baruch Hashem*, but there are two important things that I need to discuss with you."

The *rebbetzin* nodded encouragingly at Nicole, thinking with pride about the great strides this young woman had made since she had left the convent. Nicole had converted only a few months before and everything had been going smoothly since then. "What is on your mind?"

"Well," said Nicole, "first of all, I'm certain that my father knows I have converted. He is not the type to just let go, as you've no doubt realized. I've even noticed, once or twice as I was out walking, a familiar face here and there, sometimes from a car driving by or at a bus stop across the street. I am definitely being watched and they know what I'm doing."

The *rebbetzin* admired Nicole's coolness as she imparted this bit of information. "Do you want to bring this to the police?" she asked, her voice a little uncertain.

Nicole smiled. "To these men, any kind of security would just be a joke. If my father decided that he wanted me home, I would be home by now. Obviously, he is hoping that I'll come home on my own. I just thought you should know about the surveillance."

She lowered her voice as she continued, "There is also something else I wanted to discuss with you. I would like to start looking to get married."

"What!" The *rebbetzin*'s eyes widened. "You've only been Jewish a few months, and you're just barely twenty years old, Nicole. What's your hurry?"

"Let me explain," continued Nicole, unperturbed, "and I think you will agree with me that now is a good time to start looking.

"When I was twelve," she said, looking directly at the *rebbetzin*, "my father and I went to Sicily for a vacation. We stayed in his boyhood village with my grandmother, and we had a wonderful time. It is so beautiful there — you have to see it to believe it.

"We went for long walks in the forests, ate all the native foods, and went horseback riding. Unfortunately, the trip was not uneventful.

"A week after we arrived, my father asked one of his childhood friends, a man by the name of Sylvio, to drive me around and show me the sights. We saw the quaint villages with their beautiful meadows and fields of flowers. Fountains sprayed the air with their cooling spray. I was shown all the tourist attractions, the ancient ruins, the superb architecture.

"Sicilian country roads are beautiful, but they can be very dangerous, especially since Italian drivers take them at high speeds. Rain had fallen the night before, and the road was slick. Sylvio took a curve too fast — and we were plunging over the edge, down a steep mountain.

"When I regained consciousness three days later, I found myself in a small Sicilian hospital. Over the next months my father saw to it that I had the best treatment available, the top doctors. My wounds healed and eventually I was able to walk again. But there'd been internal injuries, and once I was stronger the doctors told me the terrible truth — I would never be able to have children."

Nicole spoke in a low, measured voice, keeping all emotion carefully controlled. "For years I wondered what the purpose of my life was, why I had to suffer so. The priests and nuns could never answer my questions. Only here did I finally begin to understand. Hashem must have something for me to do with my life. And since I am a convert and I have a physical problem, I think it would be wise to start looking into my prospects for marriage now."

The *rebbetzin* gazed at her compassionately. Clearly, this young woman had faced her challenge with courage and grace. Meaningless words of sympathy had no place here. She put a warm hand on Nicole's shoulder. "Hashem will help," she said quietly. "I'll make some phone calls and see what I can do."

It was early spring, several months after my breakup with Karen. I leaned back in my seat in the *beis midrash* and stretched. Zack and I had just finished a tough *sugya*. We had really worked hard at it and now we were good and ready for a break. "Let's go get something to eat," I told Zack. He liked that idea, so we got our jackets and left the building.

Just as we were entering our favorite *heimeshe* restaurant, my cell phone rang. When my phone rings, I can usually tell if the call is an important one or not. I don't know how, but I can tell if it's just a friend, a rabbi, or Zack. This ring was important; I felt it.

I answered the phone. "Yes?"

"Hello, Keith? This is Rabbi Zicherman. I would like to meet with you concerning an extremely important matter. When will you be able to come over to my house?"

"Zack and I are about to eat supper; I can come in about an hour."

"Great," said the rabbi. "You know where I live, don't you?"

"Yes," I said.

"Okay, see you soon."

I hung up the phone and turned to Zack. "Things are happening."

Rabbi Zicherman led me into his simple apartment, his face lighting up the room as much as the lightbulbs hanging from the ceiling. He ushered me into his study, making certain I was seated and comfortable before he himself had a seat.

"As you know, Keith, the position you are in is not the most enviable one. I'm sure there are times when you are ready to give up the fight and lay down your weapons. *Baruch Hashem*, you have Zecharia to encourage you when you're feeling down.

"On the whole, marriage is a problem for you. However, there are certain people who do meet the qualifications you need in order to be able to marry. This morning I received a most interesting phone call from Rebbetzin Greenberg over at Ahavas HaTorah. about a very fascinating young lady who is currently studying there. She converted not too long ago and everyone there has the greatest respect for her. Now, Keith, a convert is permitted to marry a *mamzer*. However, there is an additional problem, which is that any children you have would be born with the same blemish you have, and the rabbis do not desire that we add additional blemishes to *klal Yisrael*."

I listened very nervously, not knowing exactly where this was headed.

"In this particular case," continued Rabbi Zicherman, "should you and this girl get married, you would not have such a problem, since she too has a challenge to overcome. From what I understand, she is unable to have children."

My jaw dropped. "You want me to marry a girl who cannot have kids?" I asked in disbelief. I tried hard to keep my voice from rising. "What should I get married for? To come home to an empty house for the rest of my life? Do I come across as a person who doesn't want to raise children? You know that the Torah views having children and giving to them as one of the greatest accomplishments of a person's life, and you expect me to just give it up?"

Rabbi Zicherman looked at me with empathy, stroking his long white beard until I ran out of steam. His eyes reflected absolute sincerity as he said, "Please allow me to explain a few ideas to you. Everyone comes down into this world with a different package. Some people are born into wealth, some are not. Some are given physical strength, some are very sickly. All sorts of various scenarios happen to people. Much of what occurs has to do with what a person did in his previous life. He might have to return to this world to fix a specific deed he didn't perfect the last time around.

"Many people succeed in raising beautiful children. But there are people," here he paused and sighed deeply, "who, *nebach*, don't get to see their children grow up, and vice versa, children whose parents pass away early on. In those cases, we wonder, was it perhaps that the child or the parent finished his job here on earth and was thus able to ascend to where his soul craved to be?

"As to those special people whom Hashem does not see fit to bless with offspring, maybe, just maybe, they have raised children! Beautiful children, but in a different generation. They returned to this world only to perfect some other characteristic preventing them from attaining their place in the next world. Having children, although extremely important, is not the only reason for getting married, Keith. Many of our biggest *gedolim* weren't *zocheh*. Their response was to go out and accept the whole Jewish world as their family."

Rabbi Zicherman went on to describe the beauty of marriage, the perfection a husband and wife could attain with the proper degree of holiness in the house.

I looked at him. "Rabbi Zicherman, how are you able to describe the life of a childless couple to such a great degree? You sound as if you're positively sure about what you are saying!"

"Perhaps you don't know it, Keith, but my wife and I have never been blessed with children. I know what I am talking about from personal experience." His eyes sparkled, and he put his arm around my shoulders. "I hope you'll give this offer the consideration it deserves."

I called Rabbi Zicherman back later that night for details. Apart from the obvious medical problems, the girl being suggested sounded very special. Converting to Judaism after months spent in a convent is an incredible achievement. She could have stayed in her world and become a nun, where not having children is part of the job description. Yet she chose to become Jewish. After speaking it over with my *rabbanim* and even going to one of the *gedolim* for an *eitzah*, I made the decision to meet Nicole Salvador.

We met at the Central Bus Station, destination Netanya. I had had enough of lounges, and besides, almost everywhere a person might go on a date in Jerusalem brought back memories of my dates with Karen. I wanted to give this *shidduch* a good chance of succeeding, without a sense of remorse over what could have been.

Nicole was waiting at the Netanya bus stop on the third floor, dressed casually in a white sweater and a denim skirt, perfect for a day on the promenade. This wasn't like an ordinary first date, for one simple reason. We both didn't have too many options, and if we could find some common points we wouldn't be too quick to overlook them.

We got to know each other pretty well on the bus ride, and by the time we had reached Netanya we were having quite a good time. It was nice to be in Netanya, a city I had not visited for a very long while. We strolled down the sunny street. The day was perfect, not too cool and not too warm, and we window-shopped.

Nicole told me her background, not withholding anything. She was concerned that I would be repulsed by her father's profession, but she was so obviously the antithesis of her father that she need not have worried at all. We took a leisurely walk down through the pedestrian mall, which was not too crowded.

At the end of the mall sits one of the finest kosher restaurants in Israel, Apropos. Everything about it is unique, from its architecture to its splendid view. That was where we went for lunch.

I requested a table overlooking the ocean, and we were seated in one of the restaurant's many nooks. The view was fantastic. Far down below we could see people on the basketball court playing ball and others drinking at the cafés that lined the beach.

One of the great sports attractions available in Netanya is hang gliding. Sitting up where we were, we could clearly see the hang gliders as they glided in the wind, high above the ocean, graceful as birds in flight.

Watching the foamy waves crashing against the rocks, we could see a cute little sailboat out in the distance. I told Nicole about my sailing competitions, and how I still missed the open water, the solitude, the quiet, and the sheer awesomeness of the universe that I had felt every time I was out on a boat.

When we finished eating, my eyes fell on a white piano near the entrance to the restaurant. No one was playing it. I asked permission to use it and the manager agreed. Sitting down on the bench, I flexed my fingers to get the playing feeling back into them and began to play a slow, heartfelt melody.

The piano was well tuned, and the acoustics in the restaurant were excellent. The music reverberated through the entire restaurant, casting a spell over the diners and waitresses. I enjoyed myself for a few minutes, losing myself in the music.

We left the restaurant and turned left onto a path that lies above the ocean, with a view that only a master artist could conceive of. Brilliantly colored flowers and shrubbery lined the path. Far beneath us the tide played games with the sand, shifting and molding it, with the willfulness of an angry child. We walked mostly in silence. It was just the time and place for a pleasant companionable stroll.

At 3:30 we went to catch the bus back to Jerusalem. It had been a phenomenal day! I couldn't help thinking about Karen a little, but it seemed like that wasn't meant to be. This, however, had a chance, or so I believed.

At five-thirty that evening, Kevin, who had been following Nicole and the boy she was seeing all day, got on the phone with Derek, instructing him to meet him at the Central Bus Station in Jerusalem. They got into their rented car and followed the boy's bus as it headed toward the Old City. They watched the boy get off the bus, and Derek got out of the car and followed the boy on foot until he reached his school. "He won't be too difficult to take care of," they told each other with knowing looks once Derek was back in the car. But now it was time to go home.

They drove home and made plans for the next day based on the Bulldozer's orders in case of the eventuality of Nicole meeting a Jewish boy. "No rough stuff," he said, "just some solid harassment. Make him understand in a reasonably painless way that it wouldn't be in his best interest to continue seeing this particular girl. Get the point across nice and clear."

Chapter Eighteen

The street outside my building was deserted when I made my back to my yeshivah the next night. It was ten o'clock and I was coming back from learning with Zack. The entire area was shrouded in darkness except for the entrance to the building, where a lone lightbulb hung, casting out its spark.

There was a man standing just outside the circle of light. He was clad all in black, from his turtleneck to his sweatpants to his sneakers. Something about his stance conveyed sinister intent. There also appeared to be something in his hand, which, although I was not too close, looked suspiciously like a weapon of some sort. I slowed my pace, considering what to do. I took my cell phone out of my pocket and flipped through it until I reached the number of one of the older boys in the yeshivah.

The man watched me, and as I started to dial he made his way toward me. He had short black hair and from his dress he looked like an assassin or specially trained marine prepared for night combat.

As the phone rang, I hoped desperately that Jake was in yeshivah tonight and that his cell phone was on.

He answered on the third ring. "Jake here."

"Jake, this is Keith. There's a dangerous-looking guy outside the building and he's heading straight towards me! Get outside quickly!"

"I'm on my way," said Jake.

All this time the man was closing the distance between us. He was now only twenty feet away, and I could see his intense blue eyes looking at me.

"Stay where you are," he yelled at me.

The last thing in the world I was going to do was to stay where I was. Hopefully, Jake and the boys would emerge soon, but I was out of here.

I took off in the opposite direction, my shoes thudding as they hit the pavement. I heard him curse in frustration as he started to chase after me. His rubber-soled shoes were soundless.

I was being pursued on an uphill path, and before I knew it I was out of breath and my heart was beating so loudly that it sounded like a bass drum. Perspiration trickled down my scalp to my forehead and then into my eyes. A strong breeze was blowing against me. I could hear Jake and the boys streaming out of the yeshivah at the end of the block, and I knew they wouldn't be able to help me. My nemesis was getting closer.

"Stop, you!" he yelled at me again. I had no intention of stopping. I continued to run, thinking to myself how strange it was that he had an English accent. I raced through alleyways, cut through courtyards, and emerged on a little cobblestoned path built on a steep incline. He was rapidly catching up — I had to make a move!

I knew there was an old house that was being renovated further up on the right. In front of it, amongst a pile of garbage that the workers hadn't as yet removed, stood an old boiler that had been taken down from the roof and replaced.

Without stopping to look at my pursuer, I tipped the rusted metal boiler over on its side. It was extremely heavy, and normally I would never have been able to move it by myself. However, this was not a normal time. It fell to the ground with a huge crash and started rolling down the cobblestoned path directly at my pursuer. I could see his eyes widen in disbelief as he realized a giant rolling pin was headed in his direction.

It was gathering speed rapidly. At the rate it was going, and with its height of two and a half feet all around, I very much doubted that my man in black would be able to jump it!

The boiler clattered down the path, its length filling up almost all the space between the houses which lined either side of the path. I saw the terror in his eyes as he turned around and started to run in the opposite direction. His only hope was to reach the end of the street before the boiler hit him. Suddenly, he lost his balance and went sprawling to the ground.

He was curled up in a ball, obviously in pain, but with the boiler almost upon him he didn't have the luxury of lying there until he felt well enough to move. He sprang to his feet and pressed himself against the wall as the boiler rolled furiously past him, missing him by an inch. It continued all the way to the end of the street, where it hit a wall, bounced off, hit the other side, and finally come to a halt in a big puddle of water, spraying dirty brown liquid in every direction. My would-be attacker collapsed once again.

I wasn't about to find out how he was doing. I quickly made my way back to the yeshivah, fervently hoping there would be no additional surprises awaiting me. As soon as I entered the building, I headed to my room, got out of my perspiration-soaked clothes, and showered, trying to make sense of what had happened.

Should I go to the police? But what could I tell them — that a man dressed in black had started chasing me for no reason at all? They'd laugh in my face and tell me to come back when I had something concrete to report.

But the episode really bothered me! Why would someone come and chase me with clear intent to do me harm? It just didn't make any sense! Unless...a crazy idea occurred to me. Looking back, I wish I had taken myself a little more seriously, but then again, everything becomes so much clearer in hindsight.

FROM: Kevin DeMartino
TO: Mr. Salvador
SUBJECT: Special Assignment Ordered by Mr. Salvador
I sent Derek to apprehend the Jewish boy Nicole is dating outside his school. He was unfortunately extremely unsuccessful, due to a brilliant maneuver on the boy's part. I will continue to follow up on my job, whatever it may entail.
Kevin

FROM: Mr. Salvador
TO: Kevin DeMartino
SUBJECT: The Same
I read your e-mail with incredulity! How on earth was an amateur Jewish boy able to get the better of you? I expect a serious improvement in your performance.
Mr. Salvador

On our next date, I took Nicole to a restaurant that had just come under reliable kashrus supervision in the German Colony. It had a nice atmosphere, good service, and spicy food, which I love. They also had sushi, of which I am not the biggest fan, but Nicole ordered it happily.

The combination of the ice cold beer, the soothing music, and the spicy food put us into a very mellow mood. Nicole told me about her childhood and about being brought up in one of the wealthier homes in New York.

She described the parties at the home of her godfather, Antonio; the carefully tended roses, daisies, and tulips around their man-made lake, on which swans floated gracefully amidst the bulrushes. In my mind's eye, I could see them — people trying so hard to be upscale, as if to out-Wasp the Wasps, but never getting there. How sad.

We left the restaurant and strolled down Emek Refa'im Street, which was busy as usual, and then turned into one of the side streets, where tall trees with thick trunks lined the narrow sidewalks. We walked and walked, exploring our characters, trying to understand how we had ended up in the amazing scenario we now found ourselves. An ex-sailing champion dating the convert daughter of a criminal. It sounded like a bunch of crazy Jewish screenwriters had gotten together and played "Can You Top This?"

Gradually we came close to the Old City. Nicole suddenly looked at her watch and gasped, "Oh, it's almost eleven o'clock. I gotta run. My roommate is arranging a party for one of the girls and I promised I would at least show my face." She stopped a taxi; we said good-bye; and she was gone. I was left standing outside the wall around the Old City, and there was a little path in front of me leading up to an entrance I had never used before.

I was tired, it was late, and I didn't want to walk all the way back to Jaffa Gate, so I slowly made my way up to the end of the path and entered the Old City. I looked around in astonishment. I was surrounded by churches. *This must be the Christian area*, I thought, with a feeling of unease one can experience sometimes when alone in a deserted area. I felt as if I was in a graveyard. The tall stone edifices stared down at me as if they knew something I did not.

I suddenly sensed, rather than saw, someone behind me. It

seemed that he was following me. I looked around and saw, to my surprise, a guy I recognized. I often saw him; either passing by my yeshivah or sitting in the square outside the bank when I passed by.

I knew I had to get away from him. I broke into a run. So did he. And suddenly it was clear to me what was going on. I remembered Nicole telling me that her father would be extremely upset if she married a Jewish boy. I had asked her then if she thought he would do something about it. She looked at me as if I was nuts and said, "C'mon, he's my father; he loves me! He wouldn't ruin my happiness."

But now, running from this stranger at 11:15 at night, through the courtyards of the domed buildings, I began to think differently. Apparently, Mr. Salvador was making certain that his daughter would not marry a Jewish boy. Maybe he wouldn't have me killed, but this was definitely not going to be a fun experience.

Suddenly something whizzed past me and struck the wall on my side, splitting the stones and sending chips flying off the wall all around me. I looked back at my worst nightmare, who had a gun in his hand with a black piece screwed on to the end of it. Probably a silencer. He was shooting over my head, apparently as a warning for me to stop where I was. I ran for my life, zigzagging from side to side, while the whistle of the bullets over my head made me lose whatever sense of direction I had. *This poor wall,* I thought to myself, noticing some fresh bullet holes joining the pre-1967 ones. Suddenly I lost my balance and ended up sprawled on the stone floor, my body aching.

I heard, as if from a distance, footsteps approaching me. Without a word, I was lifted off my feet and slammed into the nearest wall. This guy was obviously serious. He pulled me up close to his face and said with a quiet menace which sent shivers down my spine, "How about rethinking the company you hang around with? After all, there are so many nice girls around and it would really be a shame for you to get hurt!" He delivered this line with a sharp jab to my ribs.

I heard the sound of a moving vehicle, and before my assailant knew what I was doing, before even I knew what I was doing, I was on my feet and running into the glare of the car's headlights.

I didn't know where I was going, but my subconscious mind took over my decision making. It directed me where to run, when to duck, and when to reach down to the ground for a rock to throw at my pursuer.

How about a geshmake Shema, Keith, I thought, and laughed hysterically.

When I thought I could not run any longer, I turned into an alleyway which led to a huge open space in the wall, which in turn led me onto the main road which hits Jaffa Gate. Suddenly, I knew where I was.

I started breathing again. There were certain to be people still milling about around here. Now there was a lot more traffic coming toward us. I ran between the cars, desperate for someone to stop and save me. The cars just flew by. My breath came in gasps. I knew that I could not hold out much longer.

Then I glimpsed the Tower of David on the horizon, and I knew the police station was coming up on my left. I started screaming frantically, "Police, *mishtarah,* help me!"

A crowd started to gather. Policemen and soldiers on patrol looked at me in surprise. Their expressions changed to concern when they heard what I was saying. "Who is chasing you?" they asked me.

I looked back, not wanting to see my enemy coming for me with his gun in his hand, but desperately needing him to be stopped. But he was gone.

He had vanished into the blackness of the night with the

ease of a bird flying off into the horizon. As I tried to catch my breath, I wondered for the millionth time why there were so many crazy happenings in my life!

The policemen took a statement from me, and I made sure to inform them that this wasn't the first attack that I'd been subjected to. They asked me for details, but I wasn't sure what to say and how much to tell them. Besides, I really needed to speak things over with Zack and maybe even with Nicole. This whole situation was getting out of hand. I felt a little better when the police promised to patrol around my yeshivah. It wasn't much, but it was better than nothing.

I called up Zack when I finally got back to the yeshivah at two in the morning, waking him up. When I told him what had happened to me a few hours before, his voice became grave and he said, "I'll be right over."

Twenty-five minutes later, he was in my room hearing the entire story. "Of course, you'll tell Nicole what happened to you tonight," he informed me.

"She'll never believe her father is behind something like this," I said.

"C'mon," said Zack. "You have to tell her. Maybe if she speaks to her father and threatens to never talk to him again, he'll call off his boys!" Zack was so insistent that I finally agreed to call.

I got through to her the next day at 10:00. When I told her it was an urgent situation, she promised to meet me right away. We met at a little deli, where I told her about my first narrow escape with the boiler and my adventure the night before, which my bruised body refused to allow me to forget. She was horrified by my description of the whistling bullets around me and became very agitated.

"I'll put in a call to New York right away," she said, "and I'll let you know how he responds."

Nicole called me a few hours later. Her voice was furious as she told me what had transpired between herself and her father.

She had started off the conversation by saying, "I know I haven't spoken to you in a long while, and I'm sure you are very hurt and upset by my actions. But you must understand that I am not the same Nicole you knew. I am aware that you have been keeping tabs on me all this time, and that you already know that I've converted; and I am certain that you know I am dating a Jewish boy.

"Do you have a problem with my doing this?"

"Of course I do," said her father.

"Are you by any chance trying to harm him so that I should not be able to marry him?"

"Nicole," her father answered, and she could hear the hurt in his voice, "do you suspect your dear old father of such terrible actions?"

"Well," said Nicole to me, "when he said those words with such innocence, I blew up at him.

"I yelled at him that he'd deceived me all these years by acting as if his business was all aboveboard and honest and that I knew that he and his buddy Antonio enjoyed convincing people to commit suicide and that I would never believe a word he told me again, since I knew that what he was saying wasn't true!

"He, of course, got all insulted, and we had the biggest fight we ever had. I called him a ruthless sinner; he called me an ungrateful, nonsensible brat, with absolutely no brain, who made crazy accusations and whom he never wanted to speak to again! Then he hung up on me," finished Nicole, and promptly burst into tears.

I comforted her a little, but all I could think was, If her father wouldn't call off his boys, I didn't know what I would do. You might be wondering why I didn't just go to the police and explain the whole story and then rely on their protection. At this point, though, having seen how professional these men were, I felt that it would be a waste of time. My only real concern at that moment was whether I was crazy for not telling Nicole good-bye right then and there. Oh, why was this all happening to me?

West Bank

In a cave that he remembered from his years of shepherding up in the hills around Jamalkia, Yassir set up his command station. There was a very respectable array of weapons supplied by his contact in Tulkarm, a month's supply of food, and a decent amount of bomb-making equipment. He was now ready to come back to a hero's welcome and start recruiting the impressionable young boys. He adjusted his trademark bandana and put his sunglasses firmly in place. The prodigal son had returned.

Chapter Nineteen

The next few days were understandably tense ones for me. I walked around with my eyes wide open, carefully scrutinizing all passersby. There was a noticeable increase in the police presence in the area and that made me feel a little better.

Winter *zeman* had just ended, and before I could see Nicole again the *mashgiach* announced that the yeshivah's annual Nissan trip was starting in two days.

We were traveling up north and would be staying at the Kinar Hotel for the first night of the trip. The next morning, we'd continue way up north to Metulla, to a place called the Canada Center. We'd go ice-skating at their Olympic-sized rink and swimming in their giant pool. That night we'd stay in a hostel not far from the Jordan River and the next morning, bright and early, we would travel to the Hermon for a day of snowboarding and snowball fights.

All of this was so exciting that it took my mind off my crazy situation a little bit. Zack had permission to come along, too, and we looked forward to the change of pace. The morning of our departure dawned gray and cloudy. We loaded the bus with all our food and gear and left Jerusalem only half an hour later than planned, heading toward the north.

Music was blasting on the sound system and everyone was getting into party mode. Out came the nosh, the books, and the cell phones with their *geshmake* games of Snake. Before long we had reached the Kinar Hotel and its exciting indoor activities.

The day flew by and soon we were in Metulla. The Canada Center's ice skating rink was way past my expectations and we had a terrifically freezing time there, after which we warmed up in the hot and bubbling Jacuzzi. This was turning out to be some trip!

Upon leaving Metulla, we traveled to the hostel where we'd be staying for the night. The hostel was comprised of rows of two-story houses with red-tiled roofs built in a semicircle around the dining room and recreation center. They sat on a hill overlooking the forest between the hostel and the Jordan River. A small gravel-strewn path led from the hostel to a place that rented out kayaks by the hour. Going kayaking would've been fun, but the place wasn't open for business yet. In the early spring the Jordan is full of melting snow which makes kayaking pretty dangerous.

I stood on top of the hill and contemplated the raging river down below for a while, until exhaustion from my long day overwhelmed me and forced me inside for a rest.

As Kevin traversed the curving highway, always keeping the boy's tour bus in sight, he thought back to that morning's shock, when he'd watched the boy boarding a big, shiny tour bus with his friends. He couldn't allow the boy to escape his clutches! He immediately called Derek and told him to pack enough clothes and food for a couple of days. Then he drove back to the apartment, picked up Derek, and raced back to the Old City to follow the bus when it pulled out of the parking lot.

Kevin knew his job, and part of that job was keeping abreast of the situation. If that meant following the boy to the other end of the country, then so be it. The boy had not gotten the message when he'd attacked him in the Old City; Derek had spotted him and Nicole in a deli the very next day. A little more persuasion was necessary.

In a way it was good that they were leaving the city, since with all the police around lately, it was becoming mighty hard to remain unobtrusive. As they rolled along at a safe distance behind the bus, Kevin and Derek were enjoying themselves, looking forward to the next stage of their adventure.

However, as it turned out, there was no real opportunity to have some uninterrupted time alone with the boy over the next day and a half. Just when Kevin was feeling somewhat defeated, the boy's bus pulled into a hostel and Kevin knew that here he'd be able to spend some quality time with the boy. The place was dark, the houses were so spread out. Oh yes, Kevin told Derek, this was going to be easy.

After supper, Zack and I decided to take a little stroll around the grounds. It was a beautiful evening, and what seemed like millions of stars shone above us. We strolled along, not talking too much, just enjoying the walk.

Suddenly Zack turned to me and whispered, "There are two men dressed in black following us!"

All my fears came crashing back at me. As I looked over at them, I noticed a wooden sign which directed guests of the hostel toward the path which led to the kayak rental place, about a five-minute walk from where we were.

This was the third time I was running into these men. The first two times they hadn't been very successful in getting their message across, disturbed by the runaway boiler and by the police. This meant that they were probably not going to let go of me very quickly if they caught me again.

I turned to Zack and frantically motioned at him to follow me. I then took off in the direction of the path which led to the kayak rental place. If I could somehow board a kayak and get into the river, they'd be sure to follow, and if they did come after me, there was no way that they would be able to reach me. I had many hours of experience with kayaks and canoes, and these guys were probably city boys with no water experience.

We turned onto the tiny path, which was barely illuminated. Bushes and trees lined the path on both sides. A sudden late-season rainstorm started, soaking us quickly. We ran along until we arrived at a huge sign that advertised kayaks for rent.

Looking behind, we couldn't see them, but we could hear them thumping along behind us in pursuit. It was only a matter of time until they closed in on us.

We ran up to the boat storage shack and removed four oars from the pile on the floor. Together we hurried to where the boats were neatly stacked one atop the other.

Zack and I untied the chord, released the plastic sheet from the top of the pile of boats and slid one off the pile and onto the ground. We were both good swimmers, but we put on life vests as a precaution anyhow.

In the distance we could see the men in the black approaching rapidly, and we knew it would not be long before they reached us. One lit lightbulb hung at the dock, illuminating the area. The men could see us clearly as we shoved our kayak off the wooden board that led into the water and were quickly carried away by the current.

I could only hope those two city boys did not know how to kayak. Knowing they did not give up easily, I could just imagine them fumbling with the boats, trying to get one off the pile without the rest of the pile coming down with it.

Since Zack and I had both gone kayaking many times before and I had so much experience with boats, we were doing just fine. We moved smoothly to the center of the river, rowing in unison, the rain sliding off our soaked clothing.

Then, all of a sudden, there they were. Two men clad in black holding on to their oars for dear life as their kayak was battered by the swiftly flowing water. The water was freezing and I knew they were not having an easy time.

There was a muffled shout as one of the men toppled overboard and the other man tried to catch him, but failed. Somehow he managed to grab hold of the side of the kayak, and his friend hoisted him aboard. Over the rushing water we could hear them shouting at each other about how they never should have done this.

The river widened considerably and the current flowed faster. Our oars beat a steady cadence as we paddled, controlling the boat's direction. Behind us the men were turning around in circles, thrown from side to side.

We entered the rapids of the Jordan River. The water level, swollen by winter rains, was very high. When the boat plunged through the rapids we held onto our oars only by a miracle. We were ready for the plunge; they were not. They went under and came up soaked, missing one oar. Down another rapid and one man flew straight overboard.

The water carried him swiftly downstream as he frantically tried to swim, to grab hold of one of the branches by the bank, even to hang on to some of the floating debris, but he could not manage to get a hold on anything! He was sucked lower and lower into the water until only his head was visible; his arms clawed at the air, desperately seeking deliverance from the watery grave. Just before he went under completely, his friend managed to grab his arm and yank him up and over the side.

We were nearing the final leg of the normal kayak route. At

the final stretch of the route, there is a riverbank on the right where you can wash up and leave the river. On the left side a rope signals the amateur boater that he should continue no more. Beyond that rope lies a dangerous rocky area and an eight-foot drop.

As we neared the final rush of water, which would take us either to the right, if we rowed hard enough, or to the left, which meant the end of the story, I could only imagine the terror and turmoil in the hearts of our pursuers, with the sky as black as could be and the rushing, roaring river an unstoppable force, an unconquerable beast. The torrents of rain falling turned what would have been a terrific ride in the summertime into a nightmare of epic proportions.

Before the last rush of water, we made a determined move over to the bank on our right and secreted ourselves underneath the overhang. A moment later they came zooming past us sideways; one hanging on to the side for dear life, the other trying to row with a single oar. They didn't know that now was the time to get to the right side of the river where the exit was. They didn't know anything; neither could they see anything because the night was so dark.

I wondered if I should call out to them and warn them of the danger, but I knew in the roar of the water and the gusting wind they would never hear me, and with only one oar they had no chance of controlling their kayak. Panting, exhausted from our efforts, Zack and I watched with a mixture of horror and relief as the boat and the men flew into the water and over the sharp drop, out of sight. A scream seemed to echo through the darkness, and then the only sound was the mad, rushing, frothing river filled with the mountains' melted snow.

Shocked, soaking wet, and totally worn out, we placed our

kayak on the riverbank and slowly made our way back to the hostel, wondering whether we should report what had happened to the police. Finally we decided not to. All we would accomplish by telling them was opening up a can of worms. It wouldn't bring the two men back to life, and Nicole would probably be dragged into the police proceedings and the publicity. When the bodies washed ashore, the police would either dismiss it as a case of two irresponsible thrill-seekers who came to a bad end, or, if the men had police records or links to organized crime, they would assume it was some kind of underworld slaying. Either way, there were no witnesses, and with our fingerprints washed away by the river there was nothing to link us to the affair.

It wasn't pleasant, of course, to be present when two human beings drowned, but these were men who were trying to murder us and it all boiled down to a matter of survival. Perhaps Nicole's father would finally get the idea and back off. I felt liberated and quite free of fear, despite the gusts of wind and the rain swirling all around us.

The next morning dawned with a drastic weather change. Instead of gray dismal clouds, the sky was blue, with wispy white clouds lazily floating up above. We drove up to the Hermon and spent the morning unwinding from the tension of the night before.

Every time I thought about what had happened, I felt mixed feelings. On the one hand, I was very happy that the two men wouldn't be bothering me anymore, but I did have more than a touch of sympathy for them, going down the waterfall like that.

At two o'clock we took the cable cars down to the bottom of the mountain, and then we returned to Jerusalem through the Jericho Valley. We reached my yeshivah at 6:30. I went to sleep early that night and slept nine solid hours, waking up rejuvenated.

That next day, I received a phone call from Nicole, who asked me to meet her for lunch, since she had something very important to tell me. We decided to meet at Jerusalem's rose garden, a fairly private place. I didn't know what Nicole wanted to tell me, but I had a bad premonition about the whole situation.

An hour later we were sitting together on a white bench under a wooden pagoda in the rose garden, at a spot which afforded us a spectacular view of the garden's pond.

Nicole greeted me with a distant look on her face. I tried to tell her about my trip up north, not mentioning the drowning, of course, but she hardly responded. Feeling restless, I bent down to the gravel-colored ground and picked up a few pebbles to toss into the lake.

After a few minutes of silence, I finally told Nicole to just come out and say whatever it was she wanted to tell me. She nodded in agreement. "Well...I.... You see, Keith, it's like this.... Oh, I don't know how to say this! But I need to say it. I.... While you were gone I did a lot of thinking and I've decided that I need to...to break off our relationship."

"What?" I said.

She held up a hand to stop me. I could hear the misery and regret in her voice as she continued, "Since my father is such a vicious man who terrorizes anyone who gets in his way, I think it's my obligation not to endanger you any longer. Don't you understand, Keith?"

What I didn't understand was how she had reached this decision without even knowing of my close escape on the Jordan river!

How I pleaded with her! I begged, got down on one knee in supplication, and even cried! I told her that I could take care of myself. We'd go to the police, I declared! But it was all to no avail. I was being turned down. Maybe what she was doing was for my good, but I was willing to take the risk. However, no amount of pleading on my part made any impression on her, and I felt my soul splinter and crack as she apologized for the last time.

With nothing left to say, I walked her out of the garden and signaled for a taxicab. It took a while until one came, but that was okay with me. I would've happily waited forever. But then a taxi came screeching around the bend and pulled up right next to me. I opened the door for Nicole for the last time. She looked at me, her eyes filled with unshed tears, and said the two most horrible words the English language has to offer. "Good-bye," she whispered, "good-bye."

Chapter Twenty

At that moment I lost my will to live. There was no joy in my life; there would never be any happiness for me, and any effort I might expend in that direction was pointless. Good-bye, dreams of a happy home; good-bye any hope for marriage; hello sadness, loneliness, and the feeling of being a ship lost at sea.

Was this my lot in life, to be tossed from wave to wave in an endless storm? I had had enough. I was out of here. Zack tried his hardest to persuade me to stay and so did Rabbi Shiner, but I was finished. I had gone through too much, too fast, and my brain had a serious case of overload. I wasn't interested in their arguments. "Yes, you're right," I told them. "God is kind and everything He does is for the best, but I feel like an empty shell, drained of everything inside."

I changed my phone number, giving my new one to no one, not even Zack. I apologized with all my heart for not giving it to him, but I was severing all ties to everything and everyone I had known these past two and a half years. My mother would have been thrilled had she known, but she would not know. Nobody was going to know what had happened to Keith Caseman. He was going to disappear; find himself a nice empty beach and

ponder his life as the shadows of the nighttime kept him company. And he was going to regrow his hair. Welcome back, Keith; where have you been?

The night before I left, Zack and I went out to dinner at the Renaissance Hotel. We sat at a corner table, the strings of lights that hung like curtains on the windows comforting me with their warm glow. We reminisced about our friendship over the past two and a half years; the intense learning we had shared and the bond that had been created between us.

Afterwards, we left the hotel and strolled down the wide boulevard to Bayit Vegan, walking aimlessly, feeling that this walk signified the end of an era. This was the joy of friendship; the power of David and Jonathan, the type of relationship that books are written about. If I lived another three hundred years, I would never be able to find a friend as sincere, or as wise, or as special as Zack.

He begged me to reconsider my decision. What was I hoping to find, to accomplish, by setting off by myself, leaving behind all the people who loved me so much? I had no answers to his queries; and, even if I had, I was too choked up to get the words out of my mouth.

We stood on a spot overlooking the highway that runs beneath Bayit Vegan. The cars' headlights sparkled like diamonds in the inky blackness of the night. I turned to Zack and said, "Life is like a highway at midnight: always dark, except for an occasional pair of headlights passing by. That's what my life is like. Always dark and dismal, except for those few moment of joy when there is hope for something better. But then, of course, the headlights speed away and become dim with the passage of time. The same goes for my joys. They also evaporate, just melt away, until nothing remains."

Zack looked at me and said, "Until you came along, I never had a real friend. You were the first friend I've ever had and I'll never cease thanking Hashem for leading me to take refuge in your yeshivah on that rainy night so long ago.

"I bought you a good-bye gift," he said, reaching into his pocket and taking out a beautiful leather wallet. In the picture frame in the inner flap there was a terrific photo of the two of us, dressed up on Purim the year before.

"That's for you to always remember the great times we had," Zack said. "There's also a *Tefilas HaDerech* inside for you to say when you travel." He placed his hands on my head, as if he were my father, and intoned the priestly blessing, "*Yesimcha Elokim....*" Finally, we gave each other a bear hug. I was leaving, but deep in my heart I knew that Zack and I were going to be together again someday. It might not be tomorrow or next week, but there was no doubt that our lives were forever intertwined.

Eilat

I had missed the water very much. I had not realized to what an extent its absence had affected me. I swam and boated and enjoyed the sunlight, the warmth, all of which helped to dispel the coldness of the Jerusalem stone which had accumulated in my bones. The heat of Eilat was like a delightful comforter on a freezing night.

I got a job working at the aquarium on the outskirts of the city, where I did anything and everything that needed to be done. I cleaned out the tanks of the tropical fish and made certain they were fed on time, buckled people into their seats at the oceanarium theater on the premises, helped out at the snack bar, and was always ready to take an extra shift.

Most of all I enjoyed working in the jewelry shop, which was located inside a tower at the end of the aquarium. The tower's lowest level had glass windows in the walls which looked out into the Red Sea, where multicolored tropical fish in all shades of the rainbow could be observed, swimming about among the coral. On the next level, one entered a carpeted jewelry shop, where exquisite goods were beautifully displayed in shiny glass cases.

There were filigree gold necklaces, dolphin-shaped pendants, coral earrings, and rings set with semiprecious stones. I would arrange the displays, set up the new merchandise in the cases, check sales, and vacuum the carpet. After a while, the management started taking notice of my dedication to my job, and I was promoted. I truly enjoyed my work and threw myself into whatever tasks were asked of me.

During the day I was able to occupy my mind with my work. At night, though, I would stand on my porch and look out at the Red Sea and listen as the waves crashed into the huge boulders which lined the beach. My mind would fill with images of the Jerusalem world I had left behind. I tried to shake those thoughts. Angrily, I would toss my head from side to side, as if that would help me remove those bothersome memories. I knew, however, that it was futile. After a while, I would give up and go back into my room, where I would turn on the TV and try to lose myself in the world of nonsense being shown there.

Eventually, when my eyes grew too heavy, they would simply shut on me. My sleep was never peaceful and was continuously disturbed by my dreams. In the morning I often awoke with my face streaked with tears.

Jerusalem

Once you've seen a movie in color, chances are black and white won't do it for you anymore. That was exactly the way Nicole felt. For a while, she had been living in technicolor and the world had shone with brightness. After telling Keith good-bye, everything had faded to a dreary and dismal gray. She tried telling herself that it was all for the best, but she soon gave up. What was the use of going on like this? she asked herself. But on the other hand, how could she subject Keith to the constant danger of her father?

It really boiled down to the man in Manhattan who was behind all these problems and who needed to be told in no uncertain terms that nothing he could do would change her mind! Maybe he didn't realize just how serious she was about the change in her lifestyle. Now was the time to tell him, to show him, who she had become. It would be his decision. If he wanted to accept her for what she was, then maybe they would be able to have a relationship once again. If he couldn't come to terms with the new her, then it would be good-bye forever!

With these thoughts in mind, Nicole Salvador decided that it was finally time for her to go home.

West Bank

In the hills which rose above the village, Yassir assembled all the young boys who were impressed by his outlook and silver tongue. He started off their training by teaching them how to use different weapons, lining up rows of smaller stones on bigger boulders for the boys to practice sharpshooting. Yassir kept up a steady stream of comments, continuously strengthening their resolve, praising their abilities, and telling them stories from his personal experiences in Lebanon. Instinctively he knew which of the boys had a future in the field of martyrdom. Many of the boys loved what they were hearing. Some, however, resisted, and for them Yassir had to come up with a different style of persuasion.

The day had yet to dawn as the three boys made their way across Jamalkia's moonlit paths. They met Yassir down at the bottom of the village near a path which led to a shortcut through the forest. The four of them walked down the path and through the shortcut, emerging about twenty feet away from an old and rarely used piece of highway. Yassir put a finger to his lips each time one of the boys asked where they were headed.

Ten minutes later a car, its headlights off, approached from the mountain road near them. It pulled up next to them, and Yassir motioned for the boys to get in. They drove for a couple of hours, passing through a few heavily guarded checkpoints with ease.

Eventually the sky began lightening and they could see that they were approaching a big city. Near the entrance was the most daunting roadblock any of the boys had ever seen, manned by heavily armed Israeli soldiers in thick green military jackets.

After being subjected to a very tough security check, they were finally allowed entry into the city.

"Where are we, Yassir?" asked one of the boys as he took in his surroundings.

"Ali," answered Yassir, "we are in the king of Arab cities here in Palestine. We have now reached Gaza!"

It was not for nothing that Yassir had chosen that day for a visit to Gaza. Today was a most special day, a day for standing tall and proud as Arabs should. Thousands of men and boys were coming together today for a demonstration against the Israelis. Members of Hamas, Islamic Jihad, and Fatah would all stand and rally as one today, laying aside, at least for the moment, their many differences.

They exited their vehicle and were promptly swallowed up

by the huge crowd, which was steadily marching towards the square where the rally was to take place. All around them, hundreds of men, their heads wrapped in the traditional checkered head scarf, pointed their weapons up at the sky and unleashed a barrage of gunfire, in protest of the cruelties to which they were subjected to by the Israelis.

The huge throng was addressed by one of their aging spiritual leaders, after which they threw out their chests as proud Arab men and together as one fired their guns in the spirit of brotherhood, pride, and the glory of Jihad.

From out of nowhere a "traitor" was dragged out to the crowd, where a makeshift "court" was convened. He was found guilty and promptly sentenced to death. The crowd watched in glee as the boy was destroyed by the mob of blood-crazed "freedom fighters."

Then row upon row of young boys wearing mock explosive belts and black masks came marching proudly by as the crowd roared its approval. Yassir watched happily, seeing the impact on the boys that the rally had made. From here on it would be a breeze, he was sure of it.

For the first time in its history, Jamalkia was feeling unrest among its youth. In the town square, while lying under the tall trees, in its marketplaces during the bargaining process, and on the soccer field, the youth of Jamalkia exchanged information among themselves.

They discussed the glories of Jihad, the pleasure of paradise, their responsibility to further the cause of the tigers of Hamas. The elders of the village watched all these happenings with misgiving and discussed the situation in the coffee shop; but by the time they had decided on a course of action, it was too late. Yassir had become the undisputed leader of the youth of

Jamalkia, and three of the best boys in the village had been recruited and fully trained.

The leaders of Jamalkia, accompanied by some of the strongest men in the village, made their way up to the cave where Yassir was headquartered, with the goal of forcibly removing their boys from the maniac's clutches and exiling Yassir. They were shown the way to the cave by one of the boys who had started the training process.

But when they arrived at the cave, all they found were three videocassettes neatly labeled with the names of the three boys. The videos had been filmed inside the cave, with a Palestinian flag as a backdrop. In each cassette, another one of the boys gave a farewell speech and related his reasons for wanting to become a martyr. Yassir's leopards, as they called themselves, were off on the road of destruction, the road of no return!

New York

Nicole landed at Kennedy Airport for her first visit home since she had run away two years before. Mario, her father's loyal chauffeur, was waiting for her outside the baggage claim. He was puffing away on his small, twisted, black cheroot, inhaling with pleasure as he checked his watch. When he saw her, his face lit up with a smile. "My little signora is back," he exclaimed, bending down to kiss her when she approached.

Nicole stepped back just in time to avoid his kiss and duly informed him that she didn't touch men anymore; however, she was quite happy to see him again. Mollified, he led her out to his polished dark-blue Cadillac and loaded her luggage in. Nicole sat down in the back while Mario took his familiar spot behind the wheel, and they pulled smoothly away from the curb.

On the rare occasions that Nicole had misbehaved or had disobeyed her father, the Bulldozer had addressed those misdemeanors in his study. He would sit in his leather armchair looking down at her, his eyes gray and cold like chips of stone until she was sorry. Now, too, the Bulldozer would be waiting in his study. As Nicole entered her childhood home, her heart was thumping wildly at the prospect of seeing him again.

The Bulldozer was enthroned behind his massive desk, impeccably attired as usual in a dark blue pin-striped suit and a gold and maroon tie. His silver hair had a bit more white in it than it had when she had left, and he was playing with a pair of cuff links that looked like globes. He looked up as she entered the room, and Nicole noticed a few new lines on his forehead.

"So," he said, "my daughter has finally come home."

"Yes, Papa," she said, feeling chastised, like a little girl who had done something horribly wrong and would not be able to make up for it, no matter how hard she tried. The Bulldozer's voice was lower than she remembered, and not the confident rumble it had once been.

"Nicole," he said, "was I not a good father to you? Did I not give you everything a girl could possibly want? Do you know what you did to me by running away? You broke my heart! My darling daughter wasn't home when I came back from the office; in her place I found a note: 'I'm leaving — good-bye.' Is this the way to treat a loving father?"

Nicole just looked at him. "Do you want to know why I ran away, Papa?" she asked.

"Do I?" he roared. "What a question."

"Well, then," she said, "I'll tell you why."

She told him about all her doubts and questions about life's meaning over the years and how he had always squashed them by telling her that faith should be the cornerstone of her life. But then, she continued, when she had overheard the conversation between her father and her godfather Antonio that night at the party — when their talk of causing death had been so casual, she had hated him then.

It seemed to her that with all the faith in the world, if one had caused a death, then that person was a murderer. Faith and devoutness could not bring the dead back to life! If the people around her were all living lies, all pretending to be something they really were not, then she had to get out of this den of iniquity. So she ran away to settle her doubt; away from the man who was now a stranger to her.

"But," continued Nicole, "did you let me have some freedom to find myself? To develop into a person who could find it in herself to understand you? No, that you couldn't do." She pointed her finger at him. The late afternoon sun lit up the patches of dried tears on her cheeks. "Not only that; you sent your men to spy on me, don't deny it! I saw them following me around. Then you ordered them to terrify the boy I was seeing, whom I wanted to marry. And now you come accusing me, when you should be apologizing to me for your despicable treatment of me. Is that the way a father should act?"

The Bulldozer looked at his daughter intently, really seeing her for the first time. He was proud of the fiery, principled young woman who stood before him. Yes, deep in his heart he was proud of her. "Nicole, pull over a chair to this side of the desk; I want to share something with you."

Nicole did as she was bade, still wiping tears from her face with the back of her hand.

The Bulldozer took a pipe and a packet of vanilla-flavored tobacco from his desk. He struck a match and spent a few minutes trying to light his pipe. He inhaled deeply as the delicious aroma permeated the room. Leaning back in his chair, he said,

"First of all, I never intended for Kevin to hurt the boy. At most I wanted some harassment from him."

Nicole looked at him with unmoving eyes. "Regardless of what you wanted, he was quite badly hurt and it would have been much worse if he wasn't so quick on his feet!"

The Bulldozer stared at her and read much in the way she looked him straight in the eyes. He understood that she was now a grown-up, and as such would have to be treated as one. "Nicole," he said, "please allow me to share with you some of my history. Perhaps then you will come to understand, or at least recognize, a little bit, why I am the way I am."

Sicily, Italy

Benito Salvador was born in a mountainous region in the heart of Sicily. His father, Don Giovanni, had been a legend, a ruler of men, known far and wide as a protector of the poor and needy and an avenger of crimes against humanity.

Just as Benito Salvador would come to be called the Bulldozer, on account of his unique personality, so Don Giovanni's complex personality led to the description "merciful devil."

To all the widows and orphans in the surrounding villages he was a benefactor, his men bringing food to the poor and household supplies to those who could not afford to pay. In return, he expected and received unquestioned obedience. Woe to the man who overstepped the line, for as benevolent as he was, he was frightful in anger. He was the law in the region; the judge, the defense, and the prosecution.

The young Benito grew up in the shadow of his powerful father. He adored him, feared him, and loved him. Don Giovanni was the sun in Benito's world, and Benito was the natural extension of his father and was treated as such by the people in his life. As a result, Benito's outlook and character were shaped and developed by Don Giovanni.

Father and son would go horseback riding together along the mountain trails, their magnificent mounts cantering along side by side, followed closely by the don's personal bodyguard, Gino. The scent of pine needles filled the air, and the leaves crackled satisfyingly underfoot. Benito treasured those rides with his father; their conversations, the advice he was given which would come back to him throughout his lifetime.

The don discussed the business with his son, involving him in it even though he was only eleven years old. Benito knew only the kind side of his father, for he had never witnessed anything to the contrary. In all his dealings within the presence of his family, his wife and children, Don Giovanni never raised his voice. Not once.

And then one crisp autumn morning when they were out riding, two horses approached them from the opposite direction. The masked riders were carrying pistols, which they raised at the don.

Before Benito knew what was happening, his father had shoved him off his horse. The don then gave it a vicious slap, turning the normally placid creature into a crazy animal. It galloped in terror directly at the masked men.

Holding the reins in a grip of steel, the don then pulled his own horse up in the air until it was standing on its hind legs, and the bullets intended for the don ricocheted off the saddle horn.

Through all this movement, the don never hesitated. With one hand on the reins, his other hand reached into his shirt, removed the pistol he always kept in a shoulder holster, and shot one man, who toppled off his mount and over the side of the trail, far down below into the valley.

The other gunman, witnessing the bungled assassination attempt, jumped off his horse and tried to flee, but he was knocked down by Benito's runaway horse and was trampled under its feet.

The don helped Benito to his feet, put the boy in front of him on the saddle, and quickly galloped home. This was the boy's introduction to the real world he lived in. The don insisted that he watch the reprisals against those who had betrayed him. First the bodyguard, who was found hiding miles away, was killed. Afterwards the traitors in the don's employ were weeded out one by one and put to death. The don had no mercy for men like these; for them he was all devil.

And Benito learned. In the war that followed, he grew up. He witnessed bloody destruction on both sides and watched his father reward loyalty and viciously punish treachery. At the age of fifteen, he was captured while on a raid in one of the villages, which turned out to be an ambush. He and his men did not surrender. They fought like animals, inflicting tremendous damage on the other side, until the tide of the battle turned and they returned triumphantly to their village, only to discover the don's house was burning furiously.

Benito's mother, who had been living with his aunt in Palermo while the troubles were being sorted out, was fine, but his father was dead. It was only a miracle that Benito was able to escape. He made his way to his uncle's house and informed him what had occurred. Together they returned to his village at the head of his uncle's private army. The battle which ensued was the talk of Sicily for years to come.

After it was all over, there was a new don — the young, invincible Don Benito Salvador. His beautiful childhood home had been burnt to a crisp. He had a new home erected, high up on the side of one of the mountains which encircled the village. He brought his mother back to this home. Slowly but surely, he acquired a few loyal men, who respected him and followed him blindly.

And then, surprising all those around him, Benito Salvador made the decision to leave Sicily and move to New York, together with his oldest friend and bodyguard, Antonio Alfonse.

He appointed one of his top lieutenants as boss of the region, answerable only to him, but knew deep inside that the rulers in this area changed monthly. After tending to all his affairs, the Bulldozer and his best friend arrived in New York, where they proceeded to initiate Salvador Enterprises. The don's man in Sicily ruled for five months before he was deposed in a bloody coup, causing the memory of the don to slowly fade away.

His pipe had long gone cold when the Bulldozer finished his story. "My daughter, I've told you all this because I want you to understand how I can do what I do and still consider myself devout. That was how my father was and that is how I am. Please try to understand, and I, in turn, will try to be a new papa to you and accept you for what you are, allowing you to live your life the way you see fit."

He held out his arms to Nicole, who tried very hard to ignore them but found that she couldn't. She buried her face in his shoulder, smelling his aftershave, as she had done when she was a little girl. "My girl," said the Bulldozer, smiling now, "you will never know how much I missed you!"

"Probably about as much as I missed you, Papa," said Nicole. "But you must accept me as I am now, if this relationship is to work."

The Bulldozer stuck out his hand to her and said, "It's a deal. Let's shake on it. If you only knew how good it is to have you back, my child, how I now feel complete again, you would know that you could trust me now. So let us start anew, with understanding on both our parts and forgiveness for your old Papa."

Two weeks later, Nicole arrived back in Israel, happily picturing the reunion which she and Keith would soon have. As soon as she had a quiet moment, she switched on her cell phone and searched quickly in its memory for Keith's number. When she dialed, though, she was utterly dismayed to hear only a recorded message that told her the number was no longer in service.

Wondering what was going on, she dialed the number of Rabbi Zicherman, who had been their *shadchan*. She left a message for him and waited anxiously for him to call back. He finally got back to her two hours later, apologizing profusely and asking her what she wanted. She explained the situation to him, telling him how she'd made peace with her father and was now free to see Keith again.

"I'm very sorry, Nicole," he said, his voice full of sympathy, "but Keith isn't here anymore. After what happened between you, he left his yeshivah, got a new phone number, and moved out of town. I'm really sorry, but he's not in touch with me right now, and wants nothing to do with our way of life anymore.

"I tried to get his number from his friend Zecharia Bernstein, but Zecharia told me that Keith hadn't given anyone his new number, not even himself, and they weren't in touch at all."

Nicole thanked him and gently turned off her cell phone. Then, with her face as still as a mask, she locked the door to her dorm room and collapsed on her bed, where she burst into tears, crying for what she hadn't merited to get and for what could have been.

Chapter Twenty-One

The Apache helicopter lifted off from the military air base at 5:45 in the morning, Captain Mordechai Zichri at the controls. Dust flew in all directions as the giant propellers turned faster and faster, sending the giant helicopter into the sky. Mutty, as Captain Zichri was known, was as calm, cool, and collected as ever; it was, after all, his ninth mission.

He took his metal bird higher up as the rays of the sun broke through the thin layer of clouds, and Mutty thanked God for his special sun ray protectors. He checked his radar, made some calculations, and banked to the left, informing ground control of his location.

Mutty loved looking down at the scenery, of which he had a bird's-eye view. The rolling hills far down below were carpeted in sagebrush, and brilliantly colored flowers competed with each other for space. Olive trees whose trunks were gnarled with age grew every couple of feet along the way.

Mutty flew a little higher, passing over a valley between two mountains. Far down below, he could see an Arab boy shepherding a herd of sleep; most were white, but through the thick brush a few black ones stood out from the rest. The scene took him back to his childhood in Kedumim in the Shomron, where such scenes were part of daily life.

But now there was no time for fond thoughts of home; Captain Mutty Zichri had a rendezvous to keep.

The gleaming black Mercedes traversed the winding Hebron roads with ease. After only a few minutes it drove out of the city, passing through small villages where young boys were busily loading donkey carts for the morning run to the stores. Wrinkled old men in traditional white dress sat and stared into the distance, looking with interest at the Mercedes as it passed them, leaving behind a cloud of dust which took its time settling, so that by the time the air was clear the car was long gone.

The driver, a man named Salama whose swarthy, mustached face was half-hidden by sunglasses, glanced repeatedly into the rearview mirror as he kept his foot on the gas and the speedometer steady at ninety kilometers per hour. The occupants of the Mercedes had one thing in common; they were all wanted by the Israelis for crimes committed against the people of Israel. The car swept past another village, almost running over a group of black-garbed women on their way to a hard day's work in the field.

Suddenly the relative stillness of the early morning was disturbed by the muted roar of a helicopter high above. One of the worse nightmares of any terrorist was that one day a helicopter would come out of nowhere and blow him to pieces. Salama stepped down on the gas pedal, pushing the car to its limits, hoping to avoid the deadly cobra that was poised to strike.

At moments like these, Captain Mutty Zichri knew why he had been born. As he zeroed in on his target, his mind filled with

images of his brother Yair — Yair, the golden child, Yair of the sweetest voice, Yair, the good hearted — Yair, his beloved kid brother, for whom all had predicted a brilliant future. His Yair, cut down like wheat in a field while hiking in a wadi near their home.

Mutty made certain all was in order as he radioed his position to ground control and requested permission to proceed. Permission was granted.

Mutty whispered the words of Psalm 91, "*Yosheiv BeSeiser Elyon,*" with intense concentration as he targeted the black Mercedes until the computer showed the missile was locked on target. Then, humming under his breath, he pressed the release button, sending the newest technology the Israeli air force had to offer at the vehicle speeding down below. He watched as the driver made an attempt to avoid the missile, but the heat-sensing missile just homed in on its target.

The missile slammed into the back of the Mercedes, sending it flying five feet in the air and igniting it with a blazing fire. Parts of the car separated from the main body and the Mercedes rolled over, side over side, until it was resting on a narrow precipice overlooking a deep gorge. In another second its weight forced it over the side, and it toppled down into the gully. It finally came to a rest upside down, a cloud of smoke rising from its wounded body.

Mutty glanced out at the clear blue sky and whispered, "That one was for you, Yair; I hope you liked it."

The front page of the Israeli daily *Yediot Achronot* the next morning showed a picture of the twisted and charred Mercedes. Below, in individual boxes, were the photos of the occupants of the vehicle, which had been on its way to the annual meeting of Hamas leaders.

The first picture was of a distinguished-looking gentleman with black hair tinged with gray, whom the paper identified as Zair Abu Zandissi, a major player in Hamas, who had been sought by the Israelis for quite a while. The next photograph showed the driver, Salama Aldoshi, who was behind one of the Machaneh Yehudah bombings. Finally, the third picture showed one of the newest recruiters to Hamas, Yassir Badiri from Jamalkia, near Tulkarm.

The article continued with quotes from the top army brass in the Hebron region and ended by informing the reader that the three suicide bombers whom Yassir Badiri had recently videoed in his cave near Jamalkia were still on the loose, but that the army was searching for them and was confident that it would find them soon.

In a rundown home deep in the maze of rat holes known as Jenin, three teenage boys sat poring over the local Palestinian newspaper's description of the previous day's murderous attack on their leader. Yassir's leopards knew now, beyond a shadow of a doubt, that they must carry out their attacks. Now the ultimate reason behind it all would be revenge — revenge for the death of a true leader. Their resolve was firm; there was no way back.

Chapter Twenty-Two

Eilat

The tower at the end of the aquarium was, as I have already mentioned, my favorite spot in the aquarium. Now, as I completed my work for the day, I decided to go outside for a breath of fresh air. I exited through the glass doors and found myself on the balcony of the tower, a wooden-floored structure approximately thirty feet in length and twenty feet in width. A metal gate about four feet high stretched around the balcony from side to side.

I loved to stand there by myself as night descended on Eilat. The harbor lights would be turned on and the red mountains which surrounded Eilat would take on a shimmering haze in the twilight glow of the evening. I leaned against the metal gate, my hair, long once again, blowing in the ocean's breeze. Gradually the darkness took over, and the water, nine feet below the porch, took on the color of fine wine.

A few months had passed since my exit from the world of Torah, and my longing to return was still as strong as ever. I was fighting a battle. On the one hand, I missed my friends, my yeshivah, and the Old City. I longed for Zack, for the conversations we used to have, and my brain could not adjust to this new reality of not focusing on understanding and analyzing. I missed the passion of learning, the glow of satisfaction after a morning *seder*.

On the other hand, I was angry and deeply hurt at what life had dealt me. I felt that I had been thrown asunder by my parents and that I had been forced away from the girl I wished to marry. When I was given some sort of hope, it developed into a crushing letdown, and I had almost been killed. Hashem was hiding His face from me; it was as if I had been abandoned by the entire world, left on a desert island to remain in solitary confinement until the end of my days. It was so difficult to go on this way. I longed to return, but for what purpose? For utter loneliness? For a life of solitude amongst a sea of happily married friends?

I felt that I had to remain in Eilat where at least I had the sea for some consolation — and that was why I stood on the porch, night after night, screaming out my pain, my unbearable anguish, to the silent, churning water. I thirsted for answers to the mystery which was my life; and I wondered if, perhaps, I should just dive into my one remaining watery companion one night, when no one was around, and wait there until my misery would finally dissipate.

One morning, I was sitting in the office having a cup of coffee before I started the day's work when the phone rang. "Aquarium," I said. "Keith here."

The voice on the other end of the line exclaimed, "Keith, is that you?"

I couldn't believe what I was hearing. It was Zack! "Zack!" I cried out, "why on earth are you calling the aquarium?"

Zack related to me that my *rosh yeshivah*, Rabbi Shiner, had asked him to give a night-*seder shiur* in the yeshivah, and he had been teaching since I had left. I was happy for him and envious of the guys who had him as a rebbe, since I knew firsthand what a great teacher he was.

"Well," he said "it's *bein hazemanim* now and the yeshivah is planning a trip to the south. The boys will go hiking and rappelling near Ein Gedi, and they'll make a stop at the Flour Cave. Then they'll go to Eilat and stop in at the aquarium, where wonder upon wonders, I find my old and best friend Keith happens to work! I was asked to go along as a chaperon, so I'm calling to reserve tickets for next Tuesday at 11:00 in the morning."

"I can hardly believe this, Zack," I said. "Here I was, pining away for your company, and the next minute, you're calling me up out of the blue to tell me that you're coming down here. I can't wait to see you!" I reserved them tickets for the following Tuesday, and we said good-bye.

Now at least I had something to look forward to. That evening, for the first time in a long while, I went out to eat instead of paying a visit to my spot at the gate, in contemplation of the big leap.

I spent part of Monday afternoon planning out the special tour of the aquarium that I would present to my friends the next day. The thought of seeing Zack filled me with excitement. I went to sleep Monday night looking forward to the next day and counting the hours until I would see Zack once again.

Jenin

Their eyes burning with fervor, glowing with religious devotion, and red from lack of sleep, the three boys sat in the incense-filled room and prepared their minds for their mission.

For the past three days, they had heard the suras of the Koran which dealt with killing the infidels until their minds were filled with the glories of paradise. They were ready to go forth on the path to heaven. They had belts of explosives strapped to their bodies in preparation for what was to come.

Each knew his route, his destination; nothing had been left to chance. They had been taught how to blend in with the crowd wherever they might be, and they had enough money for any unforeseen event. On the morrow, the greatness of Islam would be revealed to all when they avenged their leader. They were to be martyrs to the cause and there was nothing more to be desired. Each was headed in a different direction, to a separate part of the country. They were aiming to go where the wrath of Jihad had never been felt before. At this time tomorrow, they would be in heaven.

Chapter Twenty-Three

Eilat

Tuesday morning dawned bright and sunny. Although it was only nine o'clock, the temperature was in the high seventies. I happily accomplished all my daily morning chores: fed the fish, made sure all the snack bars were well stocked, and cleaned the debris that had been left in the oceanarium theater after yesterday's last show. All the things I did every day, but somehow they seemed more enjoyable today.

Finally, I went to the office to await the yeshivah boys' arrival. There was a camera network system at the front gate of the aquarium which monitored everyone coming in and sent their picture to the computer in the office. I would be able to see their arrival from where I sat in the air-conditioned office. There was another camera trained on the area outside the gates and still others set up all around the aquarium. They were all essential for security purposes.

The aquarium's policy was that one of the staff had to be constantly monitoring the security system, making sure no suspicious people infiltrated the aquarium. Every new staff member was given a crash course on the security system, thereby spreading the responsibility of security to everyone and not just to a few employees. That way no one person had to sit in front of a computer screen for hours on end.

I enjoyed sitting in the office, where I was able to experiment with the new system the aquarium had recently acquired. If I saw anything unusual on the screen I would enlarge the picture, using the newest technology to get a clear look at the smallest of details. Usually, though, it was a pretty boring job, since nothing ever happened there.

This morning it was just the run-of-the-mill crowd with lots of little children out for a day of sun and fresh air. At 10:45, my excitement was growing by leaps and bounds. I decided to stay on the computer five more minutes and then go to the front gate and meet Zack there. As I watched the entrance to the aquarium, a few more people straggled in, the last one a tall, blond young man wearing a leather bomber jacket and jeans. He was about six-foot-one and twenty or twenty-one years old. I liked his leather jacket, which I could see shining in the sunlight even where I was.

Hold it, I said to myself. *What's that guy doing wearing a leather jacket when it's seventy-eight degrees outside*? He was quite bulky under that jacket too, I noticed! The situation made me a little nervous. It was time to notify security and find out what this guy's deal was. I pressed the button which was supposed to put me in contact with security and waited for them to reply. Meanwhile I watched as the blond haired man entered the gate without being stopped. I pressed the button again. No response. There seemed to be something wrong with the security radio system; I wasn't getting through to anyone!

I told myself to calm down. What I saw was probably nothing anyway. So what if he was wearing a leather jacket? Maybe he didn't want to leave it on the bus. I called someone else into the office to take over for me and mentioned that the call button wasn't working and should be fixed. Then I made my way down to the front gate, keeping an eye out for the blond guy the entire way, hoping that I wasn't making a terrible mistake by not sending security after him.

The blond-haired man was perspiring. He reached a hand up to his forehead to wipe away the perspiration, then quickly pulled it back as he remembered that he was smearing his makeup. He wished that he didn't have to wear the heavy leather jacket. Well, it didn't matter, he told himself; soon he would be in paradise where it was cool as could be, with the fountains of water forever flowing. He derived comfort from that delightful thought as he sat down on a bench to get his bearings.

His instructions were to locate the most heavily populated area in the aquarium and then to blow himself up. His mind filled with images of the white-bearded *imam* whose eyes flashed with the zeal of a true believer. "The more infidels you take with you, my children," he would say, "the greater your reward will be." Soon, soon it would happen; he would be a martyr and Arab children the world over would sing his name in praise forever.

He inspected the immediate area; there were not too many people around. He noticed some signs which pointed to the different sections of the aquarium. One sign said "Oceanarium Show," with an arrow pointing to the right. That was probably where he would find a lot of people. He had learned that the infidels were lazy, unlike the hardworking Arabs. They were the type of people who sat around and watched movies. He got up and started off in the direction of the oceanarium.

I waited by the gate for a while until the bus pulled up. For some reason I suddenly felt shy. Would Zack and I feel as close as we used to feel now that I wasn't religious anymore? I watched as the guys began getting off the bus. And then, there he was, my Zack.

Suddenly I wasn't shy anymore. I ran to him, picking him up off the ground, and holding him up in the air. "Zack," I yelled, "oh, how I missed you!"

"Keith," he yelled back, "you're looking great!" And everything was the exactly the same again.

Zack gave the girl behind the counter his credit card number. She ran it through the computer, and then I led the entire group into the aquarium.

Zack and I walked in the front of the group, together just like we used to be. "I want to take you guys to my favorite spot in the aquarium: the underwater observatory," I said. "I think that deserves to be the first stop."

"Sounds good," said Zack. "Lead the way."

We sauntered slowly through the grounds, enjoying every minute of this reunion. After a quick stop at one of the vending machines for some cans of soda, we made our way to the place I loved best, the Tower.

The blond man followed the arrow until he arrived at the entrance to the oceanarium theater. He expected to see a line of people waiting to get in for the next show. To his disgust, there were only a few tourists milling about; definitely not enough to warrant a high level of paradise. He glanced at the list of show times posted to the left of the theater entrance. The first show was to begin in twenty minutes.

One thing was definite; he couldn't wait there. He was under scrutiny already; he could feel the eyes of the people checking him out. He could almost hear them saying to themselves, *I wonder why that man is wearing a thick leather jacket on a hot day like today*. He could not afford having the answer occur to one of them. He must move on. Where to go? He glanced around, trying to appear nonchalant, and noticed a tall round building at the far end of the aquarium. Many people were heading in that direction. That's where he would go, he decided. To the Tower.

We entered the underground observatory, Zack and I leading the way. Down there, beneath the ocean, yet apart from it, we were in an exotic world with rainbow-colored inhabitants. Each individual fish was more brilliant than the next. Looking out the windows into the ocean's vast depths, I was overcome anew by its grandeur and majesty. I could sense that Zack felt the same way. He studied the scenery intently. Nothing escaped him, be it original coral structures, underwater plants, or the ocean's colors down below.

After a while, we moved on to the jewelry shop on the next floor, where some of the boys purchased gifts for their folks back home. As the guys noticed the balcony which jutted off the side of the tower, more and more of them started making their way over. Some took pictures against the backdrop of the ocean; some just stood and appreciated the view.

And then, as I was saying something to Zack, I saw him. I reached down to the walkie-talkie I had put on when I left the office and quickly spoke into it. "All security to the Tower, 10-4. I repeat, all security to the Tower."

He was still wearing his heavy leather jacket and he was sweating. As I looked a little closer, I realized it was not sweat; it was makeup. And, in the areas on his face that the makeup was coming off, darker skin showed underneath. I glanced at his eyes — they were glazed.

Our security instructors always said, "If you look at the eyes and they are blank or glazed over, with no emotions showing, then you're in trouble."

Almost all the yeshivah boys were standing together near the far end of the balcony, posing for a picture, as the blond man slowly started to make his way in their direction. I was five feet away from him. If I didn't act immediately, the results would be catastrophic.

The past half-year of my life flashed before my eyes. All the pain, the raw suffering I had undergone; *perhaps*, I thought, *it had all occurred for one reason, to save my brothers, here today*. Maybe I, who had no future anyhow, had been sent here to save all these terrific boys who did have a life to look forward to. I remembered reading the Rambam about dying *al kiddush Hashem*. I was prepared.

Swiftly, I strode over to the man. When I was behind him, I bent down in a crouch. Without any warning, I stuck my head and right shoulder between his legs and lifted him up into the air. The look on his face must have been a sight to behold as his leather jacket lifted up and an explosives belt was revealed for all to see!

Zack started running over to me. "Stay away!" I screamed at him. I rushed over to the railing, hoping to throw the terrorist off the porch and into the water before he had a chance to explode his package of death.

He tried to reach down into his pants pocket where the button to set off the explosives was evidently located, but somehow his hand got stuck on my long hair. He pulled my hair, clawing at it with one hand and slamming me on the head with the other as he tried desperately to fulfill his death wish.

I held on to him, my right arm wrapped around his legs. With my other hand, I pulled his arm down to my mouth and bit down with all my strength, sinking my jaw into his upper arm.

He released my hair immediately and grabbed his arm, shrieking in agony.

At that moment, I was able to reach the metal gate. With my last bit of strength, I hurled the terrorist off my shoulders, over the gate and into the churning waters below. As he dropped, never ceasing his agonized cursing in Arabic, he moved his blood-drenched arm towards his pocket and the button.

There was a huge explosion and the sky filled with smoke. Debris rained down in all directions. A red haze filled the air. Glass came pouring down until the porch was covered in a thick layer of sharp slivers. The water rose up from the ocean like a fountain, twenty feet into the air, joining with the metal gate and wooden floorboards of the porch.

I was left standing on a metal strut which was attached to the foundation of the porch; the wooden boards which had lain there a second ago were now gone. On either side of me there was a nine-foot drop to the water below. I couldn't move a foot in either direction. The metal gate was a memory of the past. The tower looked like a remnant of the London blitz, all the windows blown out, jagged edges of glass embedded in the door frame, making it look like a shark's mouth.

Zack and all the boys were stranded at the far end of the balcony, the floor all but missing between them and the doorway of the porch. But did that matter in the least? We were alive! I had numerous scratches from the scuffle with the terrorist and I was bleeding in a few places where the glass shards had cut me; other than that, nothing! Everyone was overcome by the miracle that had just occurred. I stood there on that wrecked porch and rejoiced!

Through the screams and the crying rose a voice high above the rest. It was Zack. He recited the *HaGomel* blessing with more emotion than I had ever heard anyone make a *berachah* before, his voice rising chokingly with every word as he concluded,

"*Hagomel lechayavim tovos shegimalani kol tov.*" Everyone answered Amen with all their hearts. It was as if the angels in heaven were conveying their happiness at our deliverance by joining their voices together with ours. I will never forget that day.

After it was all over, the rescue boats evacuated everyone to the main part of the aquarium. Some of the boys were treated for shock or scratches from the glass; some sat huddled in blankets, sipping hot drinks to soothe their nerves. Zack and I went for a walk.

"Listen, Keith," he began, "you can buy what I'm going to tell you, or you can totally dismiss it. I think the reason you had to go through all those horrible experiences of the last few months was in order for you to end up here, in exactly the right place to avert what possibly could have been an utter tragedy."

"Zack," I said, "the same exact thoughts occurred to me also, immediately before I decided to risk my life and attack the terrorist."

"Listen, Keith," Zack continued, "I want you to come back. No! I need you to come back. Please! Are you happy now that you left?"

"No," I admitted.

"Please return with us to Yerushalayim. Rabbi Shiner will be thrilled to have you back again. You'll also make me the happiest man in the world by becoming my *chavrusa* again. You have no idea how much I miss learning with you."

"But, Zack," I protested, "what about the fact that I won't have a family, unlike everyone around us? You will eventually get married, and then I'm going to be left alone. It's a terrible feeling, loneliness."

"I know," said Zack. "But, Keith, this is your lot in life, your portion in this world. I feel you're destined to be someone special, someone whom everyone will come to for advice one day. Develop your potential. Don't stifle your chance at greatness."

He spoke on and on, from the depths of his heart, with the love that only true friends can feel for each other. I cried on his shoulder. He comforted me. I told him, in bitter tones, how I felt I had been abandoned by Hashem. He spoke at length about *emunah*. I described my overwhelming terror of the future. Zack promised to stand by my side.

We spoke for hours, as the sun set above the Red Sea and the aquarium slowly returned to normal. And, finally, after being cajoled, pushed, entreated, embraced, listened to, and accepted, I let my barriers down, let his love wash over me, and agreed to come back.

Chapter Twenty-Four

Six months had passed since my return to Jerusalem, and I was doing great! Learning was going really well. Zack and I were still extremely close, still *shteig*ing away. It wasn't exactly the same since Zack's engagement and marriage. Yup, at twenty-five years old, Zack finally found the right girl and settled down. Her name was Avigail Weiss, and she was from Toronto. As much as a guy is your friend, you are bound to lose him to a certain extent when he gets married. That's the way it should be, although it doesn't make it any easier. We were still *chavrusa*s, thank God, and I had a standing Shabbos invitation to their home, so no complaints.

I was pretty happy with life, once I had come to terms with my situation. Yes, the chances of getting married were quite slim, but life has many other facets to it and I enjoyed those instead. I hoped I would end up working at something which would benefit *klal Yisrael* — maybe doing *kiruv* in some far-off place. I focused on what Hashem was giving me, and I was able to become a truly happy person. Once in a while that old depression would surface, and then I would need an emergency dosage of Zack's encouragement to pull myself back up. But, all in all, I was sincerely happy for Zack. As for myself, life was interesting and enjoyable and I was content.

On a Tuesday afternoon, at exactly 5:27, I received the phone call. I remember the time since I glanced at my watch to see how much time there was left to afternoon *seder.* I was going to ask the guy who brought me the message to please tell whoever it was to call back a little later. Before I could say anything, though, he preempted me. "I know you don't like to be disturbed in the middle of your learning, but the woman on the other end said it was very important! She even used the word *urgent*!"

Zack and I exchanged a glance. Intrigued, I left the *beis midrash* and made my way over to the row of public phones in the hallway. A voice I had not heard for a very long time came floating over the wires: my mother's. She sounded excited about something, but holding back at the same time. I had not spoken to her for a year, ever since that traumatic conversation we had had. I wondered what was going on.

"Keith," she said, "I want you to come home as soon as possible!"

"Why, Mom?" I asked.

"Don't ask questions; get on the phone to your travel agent and book a ticket on the next available flight. Call me back with your flight information as soon as you have it." And, before she hung up, she said those words I had been waiting to hear for so long. "I love you, Keith, and I missed you more than you'll ever know." Her tone of voice was so different. It was as if she had reverted to being my mother again.

We hung up. I had no idea what was going on, but I figured that she had a pretty good reason for this kind of behavior.

I returned to the *beis midrash* as if in a dream. Zack lifted an eyebrow at me inquiringly. "Zack," I said, "that was one of the most bizarre telephone conversations I've ever had."

Together, we went over to the *rosh yeshivah* to tell him about this latest development. "Well," said Rabbi Shiner, after he had heard the whole story, "off you go to the travel agent to book your ticket."

"Just like that?" I asked.

"Yes, Keith," he said. "If your mother, who was hurt, angry, and upset with you, just called you after not speaking to you for over a year, I think she must have something mighty important to tell you. Go book your flight and may the *Ribbono Shel Olam* be with you." He gave me a kiss.

The entire flight, I could not stop wondering what my mother could possibly have seemed so excited about. I could not figure it out! My mind churned with possibilities — maybe this, maybe that. Finally I turned off my brain and went to sleep. When I awoke, I davened and ate the airline breakfast, all the while not allowing myself to wonder what effect my mother's revelation would have on my life. I tried to lose myself in a book until we landed, but the truth was that I could not concentrate on a single word. I had this feeling that something monumental was in the works.

Both my parents were waiting for me at the passenger arrival area at O'Hare Airport. Not only that, but my mother also had a big welcoming smile on her face. They hugged me and helped me get my luggage to the car. It was like old times again. My father concentrated on his driving; my mother flipped through the channels, looking for a song she liked. She finally settled on "The Homeward Bound." I didn't bother asking for an explanation to this unexpected demand for me to return home. I knew I would be informed whenever they deemed it appropriate. Yet I was bursting with curiosity.

We turned right on to Route 33 and there were my oaks, back to their friendly selves, swaying to and fro, waving their branches at me in a show of congeniality. As we turned into our driveway, I could see a big sign strung across the entire front of the house. "Welcome home, Keith," it read. I was overwhelmed by the turnaround in our relationship! For over a year, not a word from my mother, and suddenly, the red carpet gets pulled out!

My mother went into the kitchen to prepare supper. She'd gone to a lot of trouble to get prepackaged kosher food and paper goods. I changed into shorts and an old "And One" T-shirt. Even though I was yawning with jet lag, I ran down the stairs in the back of the house which led to the dock, where my beloved Kelly was still moored and waiting patiently for me, bobbing up and down in the water. I ran down the dock and slipped off her ropes, and off we went. Oh, what a pleasure! To sail in my boat!

The wind was once more blowing my hair back off my forehead. It was so good to be home. Looking at the water, it seemed like I could do anything I wanted to. I had a feeling of hope and joy, a promise of salvation. I stayed out for an hour and a half, just gulping down breaths of lake air, my boat and I together again at last. All I needed to complete the awesomeness of it all was a wife to be standing next to me on the deck, while up in the purple heavens the stars came out of hiding. It would be perfect. If only....

I finally pulled myself out of my reverie and reluctantly brought my boat back to the dock. Supper was a quick affair for me that night; then I davened *maariv* and went to bed.

I woke up late the next morning, showered to clear my head, and then davened in my room. I was hopeful that today I would find out what this was all about. When I came downstairs, my mother was waiting for me in the kitchen. She was dressed in a very nice outfit and heels.

"Good morning, Keith. Please have some breakfast and then join us in the den."

I had a bowl of my trusty old Cheerios, made an after *berachah*, and then made my way to the den.

Sitting across from my mother and father on one of the armchairs was a man I had never met before. He stood up and shook my hand. "Keith," said my mother, "let me introduce you to my first husband, Kenny Gordon."

"Hello, Keith," said the man, looking clearly uncomfortable. "I have some news of the utmost importance to relate to you. Before I do, however, I would like to tell you something.

"When your mother realized what she had done to you by not making certain to arrange for a *get*, her entire life was shattered. She felt that she had betrayed you — even worse, like she had killed you. She called me up and told me the whole sorry story. I, too, wished that I could redo the terrible actions I had done all those years ago, when I had demanded an exorbitant amount of money in return for a *get*.

"I was young, immature, and very hurt by your mother, and all I knew was that I wanted to get back at her. I had no idea of the consequences of my actions. When your mother told me that you could not get married because of what we had done, I did not know what to do with myself. But there seemed to be nothing I could do. The damage was done. That is the scary part of it all. In cases like these, the damage is irrevocable."

I listened to the impassioned speech, not daring to breathe,

and wondered where he was heading.

"Well," Kenny continued, "I suffered. I really did, Keith; just knowing how you felt was enough to ruin my nights. I would lie awake, thinking to myself how, because of my horrible need to exact revenge, I had caused a tragedy. I became depressed and I didn't know how to climb out of it."

I could not help thinking how weird it was to be sitting with my parents and my mother's first husband in my childhood home, which had been off-limits to me for so long.

"Two months ago," Kenny continued, "my mother passed away." He held up his hand at me when I conveyed my sympathy. "It was very sudden," he said. "From one second to the next. It can be like that with a heart attack, you know. Anyhow, since I am her sole heir, I drove down to her bank to go over the financial documents, and I came across some very interesting information that I now would like to show you."

He reached into his pocket and drew out a faded and frayed yellow envelope, which he handed to me with a flourish. The words on the side read "United States Adoption Agency."

With trembling fingers, I opened the flap and withdrew the creased white paper. My eyes swimming with tears, I read, "The United States hereby grants custody of a Caucasian male, name of Brian Patrick McCullon, to Mr. and Mrs. Edward Gordon, on the 29th of May, 1951."

Kenny continued speaking, "At first, I felt very upset and betrayed that I had never been told I was adopted. After a few weeks, however, it struck me that perhaps I wasn't actually Jewish! McCullon isn't a Jewish name. Just to make certain I hired a lawyer, who traced my lineage right back to Ireland."

"Wait," I said. "Didn't your parents have you converted when you were adopted?"

"Sure, they did," said Kenny. "Reform. But I know the laws; I read a tremendous amount about Judaism, because of all this, and I know what the status of a Reform conversion is." He grinned. "I'm as 'goyish' as they come and thrilled about it."

I jumped up from my seat and hugged him spontaneously. My father and mother both hugged and kissed me, too. It was as if the sky had been gray all this time, and suddenly I could see the world in technicolor again! With tears streaming down my cheeks, I thanked Hashem with all my heart. Then I thanked Kenny for his trouble, clutching the envelope that I would need as proof of my status.

My mother was back! It was as if the bad times had never existed and she and I were as close as ever before. We sat companionably together in the den, the grandfather clock ticking away the seconds: She looked at me and said, "Keith?"

"Yes, Mom?"

"I never stopped loving you, you know that, don't you?"

"Of course, Mom," I said, "not that it didn't hurt."

A look of excruciating sadness passed over her face. "Keith," she said, "I hope you never go through what I went through, knowing that you had destroyed the life of your only child, with no hope of making amends. What good would my apology have done? The fact is that you felt that your entire life was over. I was so overjoyed to find out that you're a good Jew after all; a perfect Jewish boy who can marry anybody he wants." And then, my mother, my antireligious mother, said two words I had never dreamed I would hear coming from her mouth: "*Baruch Hashem*." I could see she really meant it!

Chapter Twenty-Five

We walked along the wooden pier to the sailboat I had rented for the evening. What a night it was! Millions of twinkling stars in the black sky above us reflected back into the calm, dark sea. This was the big night; the night I had been yearning for for so long. We were going for a ride tonight.

We reached the end of the pier and I spotted our sailboat among the other boats. She was a modern, gleaming, state-of-the-art sailboat; she was beautiful, and she was mine for the night.

A man and woman in white uniforms stood waiting on either side of the gangplank for us — Zack and Avigail, our attendants for the evening, their presence taking care of the *yichud* problem. "Welcome aboard," said Zack, as we stepped onto the boat. "Your table awaits you on the deck."

Together, we made our way onto the deck where a table and two chairs were set up for us. The table was covered in a regal white tablecloth and two candles cast a shimmering light on the surroundings. Karen gasped in delight. "Wow, Keith," she exclaimed, "this is unreal; like a dream!"

She didn't realize that, for me, this was a dream. A dream

come true: to be with the girl who would become my wife, on a sailboat, doing what I loved best; this was something which I had thought was never going to happen, and I was overwhelmed with joy.

I slipped the ropes off their moorings, adjusted the sails, and checked that everything was running smoothly. Then I eased the boat away from the dock and took it out to the Mediterranean. We sailed underneath a sky made to order, while dining with exquisite silverware and china, the food having been professionally arranged. Zack and Avigail served us from beginning to end, and both disappeared between courses to allow us to talk.

Finally, before I turned the boat around to return, I asked Karen to come stand with me next to the railing of the sailboat — and withdrew a black velvet box from my jacket pocket. Inside, nestled in satin, was her ring. There and then, while the wind whistled joyously and whipped our hair and the waves slapped the boat with steady comforting sounds, we became *chassan* and *kallah*, joining together to form another *bayis ne'eman* in *klal Yisrael*.

Epilogue

The bris of my son, Yaakov Simcha ben Yehuda, was held in one of the many little *simchah* halls which dot the Geulah neighborhood — the kind of place where the waiters double as the cleaning staff, and they serve up a terrific, greasy, *fleishig* meal every morning. The bris proceeded right on schedule, and I merited to enter my son into the covenant.

During the meal, I introduced my *rosh yeshivah*, Rabbi Shiner, who then got up to speak. As he spoke, I listened with only half my brain. With the other half I was taking in all the joyous faces seated around the tables. My parents were there, gracing us with their presence, the smiles on their faces stretching from ear to ear, with the certainty that only grandparents have that their grandchild is the most unbelievable baby in the world!

Zack and Avigail were there on separate sides of the *mechitzah*, but Avigail wasn't lonely. She had little Ahuva in her carriage to keep her company. All the boys from the yeshivah were there, and Shalom and Shira had arrived from Tzefas with their entire family. Rabbi Zicherman kept leaning over to squeeze my arm, his face radiating intense happiness. Unbelievably, Nicole was there also with three children in tow! Not long after my engagement she'd married Leib Stern, a young man I knew whose wife had died of cancer about a year before, leaving him with three young children, two girls and a boy. Nicole was now their mother — so she, too, had her "happy ending."

I stood up to deliver a little speech, reflecting in my mind how our existence was now complete, with a baby to light up our home. As I looked around the crowded room, my mind took me back into the past, and I remembered....

Estelle, our friendship, and those super parties; the races, the excitement and the danger of the English storm and the Swedish whirlpool. The helicopter pilot's tale of heroic decisions, the German Karl, standing on the summit of Darje in the midst of the desert, and then the ghosts of Massada. The disco boat on the Kinneret, followed by the music Sharon had played before she offered up her *neshamah* on the piano bench next to me. The sincere hospitality of Shalom and Shira in Tzefas and the joy of the enduring friendship with Zack, which began on a dark and lonely Jerusalem night, while the rain poured down outside. My almost-meant-to-be *shidduch* with Nicole and the drenching run-in with her father's Mafia boys on the Jordan River. The aquarium down in Eilat, where we were miraculously saved from the terrorist. Overcoming the brutal knowledge that I wasn't part of *klal Yisrael*; making the decision to continue to live for Hashem, regardless of the fact that I was a blemished Jew. And, finally, my triumphant victory when I discovered life once again with a letter from the United States Adoption Agency, of all things!

I saw Karen over on the other side of the *mechitzah*; she was hushing our baby son with loving little coos. The sound filled my heart with gratitude to Hashem, and I smiled to myself as I began to speak.

The challenge had been met; the *tikkun* was complete. High up above, in the vast realms of Heaven, amid the palaces of the Garden of Eden, the angels, too, rejoiced in the happiness of the moment.

About the Author

Nachman Seltzer lives in Israel with his wife and two children. He learns in a halachah *kollel* in Yerushalayim and runs a boys' choir whose first music tape is scheduled for release soon. He is currently working on his next novel.